NEW ERA

Agency Plains (1905), looking north toward Mutton Mountains
from "Little Plains"

NEW ERA

Reflections on the Human and Natural History of Central Oregon

JAROLD RAMSEY

Oregon State University Press

Corvallis

Cover photograph: 1910 photograph of the author's mother, Wilma (front cover, right) and her brother Max (front cover, left) and sister Charlcia (back cover), near the Opal City homestead of their parents, Joe and Ella Mendenhall.

The following publishers have given permission to use quoted material from copyrighted works.

> From H.L. Davis, *Kettle of Fire* (New York: William Morrow, 1959, HarperCollins 1987)
> From *Jefferson County Reminiscences* (Portland: Binford and Mort, 1957, 1998)
> From Bess Stangland Raber, *Some Bright Morning* (Bend: Maverick Publishing, 1965)

The paper in this book meets the guidelines for permanence and durability of the Committee on Production Guidelines for Book Longevity of the Council on Library Resources and the minimum requirements of the American National Standard for Permanence of Paper for Printed Library Materials Z39.48-1984.

Library of Congress Cataloging-in-Publication Data
Ramsey, Jarold, 1937-
  New era : reflections on the human and natural history of central Oregon / by Jarold Ramsey.— 1st ed.
    p. cm.
  ISBN 0-87071-557-7 (alk. paper)
  1. Oregon—History—20th century. 2. Frontier and pioneer life—Oregon. 3. Natural history—Oregon. 4. Oregon—Biography. 5. Ramsey, Jarold, 1937- 6. Madras (Or.)—Biography. I. Title.
  F876.5.R36 2003
  979.5'8041—dc21
2003013298

Oregon State University Press
101 Waldo Hall
Corvallis OR 97331-6407

OREGON STATE
UNIVERSITY
541-737-3166 • fax 541-737-3170
http://oregonstate.edu/dept/press

Contents

❖❖

For the Aunts and Uncles

INTRODUCTION

❖❖❖

IN 1934, FRESH FROM THE SCANDALOUS SUCCESSES of his *Tobacco Road* and *God's Little Acre*, the Southern novelist Erskine Caldwell traveled across America observing ordinary country people coping with the Depression and a nationwide agricultural crisis. For some reason he visited my home town, Madras, Oregon (population then about two hundred), and when he published a book of essays on his odyssey, *Some American People*, in 1935, he chose to open the book with a sketch of Madras and the country around it in the throes of drought, dust, and economic abandonment. His essay is titled "On the Range": "home" seems pointedly left out of his title:

> In Central Oregon, on the eastern slopes of the Cascade Mountains, the shriveled grass is lying on the range like scraps of steel shavings. A gust of hot wind sweeps down to earth, and with your ear to the ground you hear a sound like someone kicking rusty springs through the wiry brown grass. …
>
> You walk a block in Madras, in any direction, and you are on the open range. As far as the eye can see, the rolling earth extends mile after mile toward an infinite horizon. The brown sod is frequently broken by squares and ovals of dusty, drifting fields. They look as if they might be tumbled-over tombstones, once erected to the faded hope of dry farming.
>
> Back from the range, you are still on the range, in Madras. The man on the [store] steps has not moved in an hour's time. He still sits looking out into the deserted street. Perhaps his hair is a little longer, perhaps not, but you can't help thinking that it hangs a little lower on his neck.
>
> You raise a hand in greeting, but receive no response. You have elected to come to Madras, and you must accept the permeating silence of the range. …

I was born a few years after Caldwell's visit, and the Madras country wasn't any greener then than what he saw in 1934. It must have looked

1

like the brave homesteading era that had begun around 1900 had about played out, and all that hard work to clear and plow the land was turning to literal dust for the hardy folks still clinging to their homesteads.

Yet by the middle of the next decade, just after World War Two, the Madras of Caldwell's sketch had been utterly transformed, in a new era of irrigation. A long-delayed federal project to convey water from the Cascade foothills north and east to our country brought in new crops, and new, more productive, and more costly styles of farming. New people, mostly from central and western Idaho, arrived here in droves, eager to get in on the beginnings of a new bonanza of 160-acre irrigated farms raising bumper yields of clover-seed, potatoes, mint, and other crops that had never been attempted on this parched and mineral soil. A Chamber of Commerce was organized, and its slogan was "Madras the Green Spot of Central Oregon."

Now, fifty years later, irrigated farming is still the Main Way here and elsewhere in Central Oregon; but with dwindling markets and prices for field-crops and cattle, and crises looming over water-rights and allocations, "agribusiness" (as we now call it) is increasingly off-balance, uncertain, like a horse stumbling but not quite falling down, not yet. Looking up and around from our irrigated fields to the changeless gray hills and rangeland beyond, I catch myself wondering if, at the last, the abiding sagebrush, juniper, and bunchgrass will reclaim their own here, as they have, long since, many of the outlying homesteads. As a boy, I heard the oldest old-timers talk wistfully about riding on open range where our showcase sprinkler-irrigated fields are now, the bunchgrass so high it tickled their horses' bellies. ...

A more likely "new era" for this country, one that neither the homesteaders nor Erskine Caldwell could have envisioned, is a hectic epoch of rapid wholesale land development. And in a sense that "new era" is already upon us—late in coming, compared to what happened decades ago in California and Arizona, but then Central Oregon has always lagged behind The Times; it was, after all, one of the last American homestead areas to be opened up.

But now in earnest, real-estate developers and their political helpers are prowling the country, looking for ways to open up and subdivide farm and range acreages for "country estates" and "hobby farms," and it's anybody's guess whether our state and county land-use laws, up to now probably the most restrictive and severely enforced in the nation, will withstand the mounting pressure for development.

And not just for expensive "view property" for housing, either. As I was completing this book, a national "merchant power-plant" company from North Carolina was aggressively pursuing plans to build and operate a gigantic 980-megawatt gas-and-steam power plant on productive rangeland just north of Grizzly Mountain, about ten miles south of Madras. The plant, consisting basically of four 747-sized jet engines and steam-turbines, would use as much water daily as the towns of Madras, Prineville, and Redmond combined—and the water would be sucked out of deep wells tapping into the famously pure "Deschutes Valley" aquifers, fourteen miles to the west, and piped to the plant. The electrical power would be transmitted to California; the depleted water resources in this semi-desert country and the climate-altering emissions would of course remain with us.

In the face of such reckless development, the first lines of W. S. Merwin's poem "The Last One" take on a local immediacy: "Well they'd made up their minds to be everywhere because why not./ Everywhere was theirs because they thought so." (*The Lice*, p.10)

When a national magazine recently identified Central Oregon as "one of the last best unspoiled places in America," the folks who live here didn't know whether to be gratified by such notice, or scared out of their wits by it.

That anxious sense of our little out-of-the-way world being somehow connected to, and ultimately discovered by, the outer world has persisted for a long time in my consciousness of homeland. At some critical stage of cognitive growth, of course, we all begin to make such connections: in the third grade, my friends and I experimentally projected our addresses outward—"Jerry Ramsey/Star Route/Agency Plains/Madras/Jefferson County/State of Oregon/United States/North America/ Planet Earth/ Solar System/Galaxy/Universe …" In the same spirit, during World War Two we amused ourselves by imagining *local* enactments of the famous battles we were reading about in remote places like Okinawa and Bastogne. It could happen here! It was exciting to imagine belonging to those ever-larger domains.

But when, in college, I began to be gone from home for longer and longer intervals, and then simply moved away altogether, the habit of imagining this target-like model of my personal geography became more and more unsettling. When (or if) I ever moved back to Central Oregon, would it have already been found out and invaded; would there be anything left of the human and natural wonders that I cherished? Would there (to misquote Gertrude Stein) be a *there* there?

So in the 1980s, when the infamous Bhagwan Shree Rajneesh and his cult-followers took over the old Muddy Ranch northeast of here, and the full glare of the national media briefly shone down on their shenanigans, it felt like the concentric orbits of my world-model were short-circuiting; my homeland, once out on the rim of American awareness, was now too close to the bull's-eye for either pride or comfort. Either the Rajneeshees would buy more and more rangeland, and succeed in their plan to take over local governments; or their mere presence would attract other cults.

When Rajneeshpuram at length imploded, and the Muddy Ranch reclaimed something of its old solitude, I recalled what an old-timer had told me, reassuringly: "Don't worry, Nature will run its course." At the time, I thought he meant "nature" in the sense of some punitive natural disaster, a cloudburst and flood or an earthquake; as things turned out, he probably meant flawed human nature, flying to pieces in the moral vacuum of a cult. Maybe—he was a very deep man—he meant nature in some inclusive ecological sense.

At any rate, the sanyasins and their loony "developments" and armed guards are long gone, leaving Muddy Creek alone to perform its daily summertime miracle of flowing briskly at night and turning to dry sand and dust in the daylight. But it was a narrow squeak for some of the most beautifully desolate land in Central Oregon, and when I visit over there now I think of Alexis de Toqueville's hair-raising observation in his *Journey to America* (1829).

> It is this consciousness of destruction, this *arrière-pensée* of quick and inevitable change that gives, we feel, so peculiar a character and such a touching beauty to the solitudes of America. One sees them with melancholy pleasure; one is in a sort of hurry to admire them.

❧

THESE ESSAYS WERE WRITTEN OVER MORE THAN A DECADE, for a variety of occasions, some academic, some otherwise, and no doubt their variations of style and tone say as much. So be it. But from the first-written essay ("New Era") on, I've been conscious of writing toward an eventual book: not a systematic history of the region, but rather a book of interrelated essays, each one an attempt at a fresh start and a new angle in an ongoing exploration of the interplay of human and natural history in Central Oregon.

My title, *New Era*, comes from the name of our little country school, and if it catches a sense of the indomitable optimism of the homesteaders who established it for their children, I also want it to suggest my concern throughout the book with changes in the land, and with what can get thrown aside and lost in the name of newness and progress. As it happened, New Era School itself was a casualty of change: the first human institution in my tender experience to be put aside for something bigger and (presumably) better—going to school in town.

If I'm nostalgic about that little school, and the whole homesteading period it symbolized, I've learned over the years, I hope, to accept and embrace most of the drastic changes here that followed the advent of irrigation. The good folks who "came with the water" (as we used to say) were authentic pioneers in their own right, bringing to this region new farming skills and a fierce determination that changed the landscape just as much as the heroic grubbing and plowing of their predecessors, the homesteaders.

One of my parents' closest friends, the late C. S. "Chet" Luelling, has left a unique personal account of the historic moment in 1948 when the new life of irrigated farming arrived on what had been his dryland fields. What to do with all that intractable water, coming at night, after years of trusting, perhaps praying, that some rain would fall on one's crops, at the right time! Chet Luelling, like many farmers I've known, was a sensitive but unsentimental man, and his account balances his regret over losing the old order of things, and his appreciation of what was replacing it under the wide Central Oregon sky. The battle to make a living at farming here would never be the same; it would be a new kind of striving, full of unheard-of risks, but maybe full of new promises too. Honor the past; on with the new!

> We stayed up until about two a.m., when the water seemed fairly well under control. I awoke around daylight to find that the ditch had broken and the water was running uncontrolled down the field past the house. I worked several hours to again get the water running in a more orderly fashion down the corrugations. ...
>
> The next full year of irrigation made a complete change in the old well-remembered appearance of the Plains. Gone were the fences. The fields were cut, filled, and leveled. Not

a vestige of sage was left in the lanes along the roads.
People were everywhere. Houses appeared on nearly every
quarter-section of land, but they didn't resemble the
original homesteaders' cabins. The fields remained green
throughout the summer.

Looking ahead to this new venture, I realized that for
these strange people, the struggle for survival would
continue, only now it applied to financial conditions, not
to the raw physical privations endured by those who
conquered the sage.

Now that I have finally returned to the old ranch north of Madras
and settled in, I've been wondering whether my efforts to write about
this country will continue to be prompted by a kind of homesickness.
Amongst the many spurs to write about the human and natural
dimensions of places, homesickness is as good as any, I suppose, if one
doesn't get carried away by it. Maybe *topophilia* more accurately describes
what I feel, especially now that I'm physically back on the scene—but
like most people I can feel pangs of something like homesickness about
remembered places that *aren't* home at all: certain out-of-the-way locales
in upstate New York, the eastern Sierras, the west of Ireland, and so on.
Maybe this feeling is as much a yearning for times lost as for places
distant.

But now that I'm back here and rediscovering certain essential facts
of this locality, like the adjustments of the meadowlark's song from season
to season, and the smell of rangeland after a shower, I find that I am
conjuring more than ever with that old "target" emblem of location. I
know, having been out in the world a little, that Central Oregon is not
really the "center" of much of anything. Most of the time (happily!) it
seems to ride on some outer orbit, around the ultimate intensities of the
great Center. Astronomers tell us that our solar system is located on the
mere peripheries of the home-galaxy, which has a colossal Black Hole at
its center. ... But handy-dandy, the emblem can turn itself inside out,
and still make sense: now its center is commonsensically the home ground
under my feet, and the realm of Events and Affairs and Heroes is *out
there* in the far beyond. In William Stafford's lines from just this
perspective, "Let all the heroes go home/if they have any ..."
("Allegiances").

Handy-dandy: homeland as *both* center of the world, and its rim—never mind the contradictions. Maybe in its very contradictoriness it's a useful conceptual model of the ecological dictum, "Think globally, act locally." In any event, it's a mental geometry that has occupied my mind all through the writing of this book, and I hope that in my explorations of the human and natural stories of one small, remote, beloved place it has helped to keep me aware of important connections between my local subjects and the great world (wherever it lies). Trying to identify and understand such connections is surely one of the defining tasks of environmental writing in our time.

WHATEVER ITS MERITS, this is an uncommonly *beholden* book. So many people have contributed to it, wittingly or unwittingly, that I hardly know where to begin, or end, a grateful list of them. Many, alas, are dead; not a few have passed on since I first took up this project. Of these I want to name my father, A. S. Ramsey; my maternal grandfather, Joe Mendenhall; my storytelling uncles Max Mendenhall and Cecil C. Moore, and my aunt Charlcia Moore; our neighbors and friends John Campbell, Chet and Lloyd Luelling, Tom Power, Eddie Bolter, Charlie Jackson; and Edna Vannoy Watts, Jessie Kibbee Sichau, Alice Florendo, Verbena Greene, Martha Stranahan, David French, and Keith Clark.

Scholars and local historians near and far have generously opened doors, shared research, drawn maps for me, including Gordon Gillespie (Director of the Bowman Museum in Prineville), Glen Love, Ward Tonsfeldt, Beth Crow, Ron Ochs, Aloha Kendall (Director of the Jefferson County Historical Museum), Mel Ashwill, Dell and Virginia Hymes, Edba Campbell Clark, Kathrine French, George Aguilar, Patty Moore Howard, Leslie Ramsey, Jack Watts, Dan Macy, Loyd Vincent, Bill Grant, Sharon Dodge, Norm Weigand, Sumner Rodriquez, and Eloise Brummer, Crook County Clerk's Office.

And closest to home, where help with an enterprise like this makes all the difference, I take pleasure in saying that I've had the steadfast support and encouragement of my mother, Wilma Mendenhall Ramsey, my brother and sister-in-law Jim and Diane Ramsey, and my wife Dorothy and our farflung family—Kate and Tim and Leo, and Sophia and Martin, and John. Without you, my dears, no story, no book!

JWR, Madras, February 2002

One

NEW ERA:
GROWING UP EAST OF THE CASCADES

EAST OF THE CASCADES AND MANY LONG YEARS AGO (at the rate
the world is changing now), before we had enough water for shade trees
and electricity for yard-lights, I could look out of our upstairs bedroom
windows at night and count on two hands the other dryland families
who lived on Agency Plains with us. Friendly yellow lights, Aladdins and
Colemans like ours, beaconing through the living-room windows of the
Evicks, the Greens, the Linkses, the Luellings, Joe Burns, the other
Ramseys; and if I looked out after ten o'clock, no house lights were visible
under the starry sky. I sometimes wondered, when did the Indians go to
bed, when they lived around here?

In the daylight, I was always impressed by the fact that Agency Plains
is a kind of mesa, maybe twelve miles long and wide, a flat little world
ringed with basalt cliffs and cut off from the general lay of the land on
all sides: by the deep canyon of the Deschutes River on the west and
north sides, by the dry valley of Paxton and Gateway to the east, and by
Willow Creek and the town of Madras on the south. "Agency," because
the western rims overlook the Warm Springs Indian Agency across the
river, where bands of Wascos, Wishrams, and Teninos were settled by the
Indian Treaty of 1855, to be joined later by several bands of Northern
Paiutes.

When my grandparents and their kinfolks arrived from Missouri in
1902 to take up their homestead claims on those western rims, a Wasco
leader named Jim Jackson crossed the river and climbed up to see what
kind of people they were, these newcomers. He returned and reported
to his sons, including Charlie (who told me the story as an old man a
few years ago), that they seemed to be decent folks, but didn't know much
of anything about the country and would probably need a lot of help.
So Jim Jackson became a regular visitor and field hand, and his son
Charlie and my uncle Stub grew up as agemates and pals, and one of
Charlie's sons, Zane, and my cousin Leslie were buddies and rivals in
high school, and another of Charlie's boys, Vern, and I were friendly in
college together, and now our two families are into the fourth generation

of friendship. When Vern got his college degree (the first of his people to do so), he returned to Warm Springs and began to make news as a far-sighted, progressive tribal secretary.

In the local newspaper, *The Madras Pioneer*, our community was celebrated weekly in a column titled "Agency Plains-Mud Springs Items," as reported by a refined old lady who was paid for her news gathering by the inch. Consequently her coverage was wonderfully thorough, right down to the births of puppies and the deaths of old dogs, letters from distant relatives and former neighbors, and weekly trips to town ("So-and-so motored to town on business on Friday, and took in a movie"). Every week the reporter would call my mother to ask for news, and if there wasn't anything to report from our household, she would invariably ask about the "doings" of other families on the Plains. My mother would always decline this invitation to serve as "an unnamed but reputable source"—a restraint on her part that disappointed not only the columnist but also my older brother and me.

As a matter of fact, gossip ran in a much swifter and freer channel than the newspaper, anyway. All the families on the Plains subscribed to a party-line telephone service, with hand-cranked battery-powered wall telephones, and wire that ran on poles, fence-posts, rooftops, abandoned farm machinery, and, inevitably, the ground. Each family had its own signal, generated by short and long turns of the crank. Ours was a *long* and a *short*. When someone called a number, *everybody's* phone rang, and we assumed that any conversation would begin with at least two or three silent listeners. This deplorable but universal practice was known as "rubbering." Some families seemed to be the subject of rubbering more than others; that was the price they had to pay, we reckoned, for living more colorful and conspicuous lives. Really extreme cases of eavesdropping could result in such a drain on the current as to render the conversation virtually inaudible for all parties, a clear case of sin betraying itself.

A dedicated rubberer could even determine the identity of a caller by the distinctive way he or she rang numbers. And of course any call that went through "Central" in Madras was *ipso facto* worth checking out, because it might be an Emergency, or even Long Distance. There was a special General Emergency number—five *longs*, I believe—which everybody was supposed to answer (like the bell in a New England village), but I don't recall that this extreme measure was ever used, not even on the day World War Two ended. We were a restrained community, and anyway, rubbering made it unnecessary.

When my older brother grew old enough to call up girls, and be called by them, the inherent tensions of such communications were magnified by the likelihood that love's shy intimacies would be shared by an invisible, uninvited, but appreciative audience. So he devised the following deterrent. He rang a girl's number one night after supper, and after all the intruding receivers had clicked on in his ear, he suavely announced like Don Ameche on the radio, "Good evening, and welcome to the Agency Plains Listening Club! We have an exciting conversation for you tonight …" and then he named in welcome four or five of our most notorious rubberers. The effect, he later reported, was like startled frogs jumping back into the pond—click after embarrassed click until the line between him and his girlfriend was free and private.

Our house sat by its lonesome at the head of a canyon leading west into the chasm of the Deschutes River; nowadays Highway 26 from Portland bends due south in front of the place. By local legend it was the site of an Indian camp; Indian friends of my father's like Charlie Jackson and Wesley Smith said so. Whenever we plowed up the garden or the hayfields south and east of the house, jasper and obsidian arrowheads and hand-sized grinding stones would emerge. Although I endorse the federal protection of Indian sites and artifacts, to this day I am unable to walk across a plowed field or even a vacant lot without looking for arrowheads—one of life's great innocent mindless pleasures, as Thoreau knew. The best arrowpoint hunter amongst us was our one-eyed cousin Billy, who could find points virtually at will, by a sixth sense he had. We all had boxes of artifacts, to be hauled out and shown to visitors from the city, and then put back. The real pleasure, as with so many things, was in the finding.

Our house was built in the early homestead years, around 1917 I believe, out of lumber made from trees that had been floated down the Metolius and Deschutes rivers to the mill at Cowles Orchard, a few miles down the canyon from our place. We were the third family (all connected by marriage) to move into it, in 1938, the year after I was born. Like most of the other houses on the Plains, it was tall, gaunt, and paintless. Seen from a distance by an outlander, it must have cried aloud for trees, and paint, and side-rooms to break up its stark lines, but such refinements were years to come. There were various outbuildings close by: a little wash-house, a garage, and a tin-roofed shop, which concealed a two-hole privy on its back side. My parents added a large chicken house, and we celebrated its fragrant newness in a world of weathered buildings by hosting a memorable dance in it. The next day we laid down straw and installed the chickens: no more dances after that.

North of the house, right on the edge of the canyon, for drainage, were the barn, granaries, and a rickety corral. Generally we kept two cows, one to milk and one to freshen; in winter, whenever it was my turn, I milked by lantern-light morning and night, teetering on a T-shaped stool and feeling heroically abused. What a medley of smells—pure essence of cow, odors of fresh and sour milk, stink of bag-balm, and redeeming it all, the mild summery scent of the hay in the mow, where no one had ever yet broken a neck jumping from the rafters.

It was much the same on every other farm thereabouts. Like most western farm communities, ours was almost tribally homogeneous; there was a Way, and we all lived it. For one thing, these families, now in their third generations, had all arrived here at the same time (my father's next oldest sister, Leda, was the first white child born on the Plains, a major article of Ramsey pride). And many of them came from English and German farm communities in northern Missouri. But why in the world did they come?

A few years ago, I visited that rich hill-and-river country around Moberly, Missouri, and went away more puzzled than ever about the motives of Grandpa Billy Ramsey and his fellow emigrés. There, the soil is black and apparently bottomless; here, it is gray, mineral, parched, and so thin over the rimrocks you'd have to anchor cornstalks with guy-wires—but we never tried to raise field-corn as a paying crop. Back there, the growing season is both long and intense, almost violent; out here, it is short and uncertain, with frost possible every month, withering winds likely every afternoon, and fifteen inches of moisture constituting a good wet year. Grandpa Billy cut his first crop of seed wheat with a hand-scythe, and Grandma gathered it with a garden rake. What did they think about their great move, as they worked through that pitiful first harvest? Grandpa Billy was already fifty-one years old; Grandma, his second wife, was in her thirties. Well, this was no paradise they'd come to, and taking dominion over all that sagebrush, juniper, and rock under that relentless sky would be the work of generations. "So be it," I imagine my grandparents and their yeoman neighbors saying, Missouri-style. "If a man can't do the job in ten years, why then let him take thirty, and raise some sons and daughters to help."

Why did they come out to the Oregon desert? For people who seemed so dour and pragmatic to me as a child forty years later, the probable

answer is surprisingly romantic. Those Missouri farmers had been hearing
for a decade that the great American frontier was closed—no more virgin
land—and no doubt they shrugged the news off with apparent
indifference, being already landed if not gentry. But when word came
back at the turn of the century that the frontier was re-opening a crack,
with lands in the central plateaus of Oregon open to quarter-section
homestead claims, the unexpected chance to wester and pioneer must
have been irresistible. They sold out and went, and learned a new life.

No doubt the late reports from the Promised Land were extravagant,
after their kind. If this was one of the last regions in western America to
be homesteaded, they found out *why* that was so soon enough, in terms
of soil and climate. But they had to come, I think. And if I can only
speculate as to why they came, I know in the bones of my heart why
they stayed, through drought and homesickness and crop failures and
the Great Depression. They stayed because the land—so bleak and austere
that even the Indians had only lived here seasonally—claimed them body
and soul.

The autumn before my father died, I took him and my mother and
my own family on a little trip through Vermont and New Hampshire,
as far as the White Mountains. Above the lovely old town of Plymouth,
surveying the hills in their gold and scarlet and enduring green, and
smelling the smoke of autumn in the air, he said, "Well, if I *couldn't* live
in central Oregon, I guess this wouldn't be bad." He was being polite, in
his gruff way, to our New Hampshire host; but what he meant, having
watched the setting sun backtracking each night along the south slopes
of Mt. Jefferson every October of his life, was that he knew something
better for himself.

IF I WERE A SERIOUS ETHNOGRAPHER, attempting a systematic description
and analysis of our little culture, I would have to pause here and offer
an account of the games, recreations, and social, fraternal, and religious
organizations of Agency Plains. It would be a brief account. Churches
we had none—the Methodists, Missionary Baptists, Free Methodists,
Christians, and Episcopalians amongst us all met in Madras; if there were
any Catholics, they kept a low profile amidst such a staunchly Protestant
bunch. Lodges, also located in Madras, were important, dividing our
families between the Masons and the Eastern Star on the one hand, and

the Odd Fellows and the Rebekahs on the other. A few families figured in both fraternal sets, which shared a dusty second-story lodge hall in downtown Madras, catty-corner from the hotel. I can still smell the dust raised on those interminable evenings, first by the new officers sashaying around the floor in close-order ceremonial drill (what my dad liked to call "threading the needle"), and then by the whole assembly, even children, dancing the night away (even until midnight), perhaps to Dan Macy's "Warm Springs Indians," featuring Gib Kalama on the piano and Henry Kalama on everything else.

The one truly native Agency Plains social organization in my childhood was known as "The Neighborly Club." In theory it included every woman on the Plains; it met at a rotation of houses on the third Thursday of every month. In our bleak and isolated circumstances, its civilizing influences were considerable. It brought rank newcomers and new brides into the bosom of the female community; it fostered the higher forms of gossiping and the exchange of recipes. And it exposed us country kids to the theory and practice of birthday parties, festive programs, and genteel entertainments, such as the elaborate Hallowe'en and Christmas programs the Club used to put on, to which even the menfolk were invited.

Once my mother and another lady presented a Hallowe'en skit for the children, in which my mother was to be accosted by the other lady, disguised as a witch. Just as the witch laid hands on her victim, my older brother, then about five, violently sprang to her defense, with hands, feet, and teeth, all the while yelling vile curses. The poor ruffled witch asked if anybody could tell her where such a nice little boy could have learned such bad language in our neighborhood. Meanwhile, my poor brother was consoled and banished to a bedroom.

By city or even small-town standards, our recreations and pastimes were few and far between. Here again, I suppose, we paid the cultural price of being a belated frontier community, cut off by one or more generations from the folkways of the "old country" in Missouri, or even the Willamette Valley. We had no fiddlers, folk singers, designated storytellers, brass bands, or social choirs; square dancing came on the scene much later, brought in by Idahoans. Our sports were noncompetitive and unsocial—fishing, hunting, looking for artifacts, sledding; I remember watching the Indians playing their intense and gregarious bone games at Warm Springs celebrations with real envy. For the women, flower gardening was *de rigeur*; men simply didn't have hobbies apart from tinkering incessantly with their machines. Neither were we adventuresome readers, although most families subscribed to *Colliers,* the *Saturday Evening Post,* the *Reader's Digest,* the *National Geographic,* and the *Oregon Farmer.* The most carefully read books were the Bible, and the "Sears and Sawbuck" and "Monkey Wards" mail-order catalogs. On our storage-battery radios, we favored gloomy old Gabriel Heatter for news, "The Jack Benny Show," and "Lum and Abner" for entertainment.

In place of formal pastimes and leisure pursuits, it seems to me, we preoccupied ourselves imaginatively with *character.* Character in the old sense of distinctive personality was our TV, our stage, our cinema and music hall, our literature. Out of the necessity of getting along with a fixed field of neighbors and relatives, rural communities like ours made a virtue, indeed a kind of art, of celebrating individual personality. I remember no conversations as animated and delicious as those in which some dour farmer's latest sayings and doings were reported and then interpreted in the light of earlier episodes. "Well, old Fritz has done it again," someone would offer. "What now?" "Well, he and the missus had the minister out for Sunday dinner, and when the minister said grace and asked for a special blessing on President Roosevelt, old Fritz, he pounds the table and says, 'By God, not in this house!' "

Rarely did such accounts aim at censure or take the form of malicious gossip. If fiction making played a part in them (as it did), it was understood as part of an imaginative and dramatic process whereby we saw someone's character becoming more truly and distinctively itself, over time. It was a little like being in a repertory theater company, where everyone was a connoisseur and a prompter of everybody else's special parts and turns, and of course everybody was also a *player,* at least some of the time. A few were extroverted enough to play themselves to any gathering at the slightest cue, but even the shyest and most stolid could be roused into self-performance with a little adroit teasing: "Hey Fritz, I hear you're praying for Roosevelt these days ..." And the fulfillment of Republican Fritz would advance a few more degrees, before our eyes.

Were these people really as colorful, as crotchety, as inexhaustibly interesting as they appeared to me as a child? Probably not, but they were all the human types we had; and what one of Dr. Johnson's friends said of him after his death—that no other man could ever remind him of the good Doctor, so unique was he—I would have to say about these characters out of my childhood. Perhaps that is just a facet of childish experience, but the shared delight in personality that made them seem like *real characters* is lacking, at least in my experience, in big-city life. It is one of the prices we pay for our impersonalized, overpopulated, and hyper-mobile urbanity, and it is a heavy one.

By the time the railroads came in 1911, life on the Plains had simplified and settled down to the mode into which I was born in 1937. Everybody had at least a half-section of land; half of each farm was summer-fallowed each year, while the other half was cropped with hard winter wheat. In my time, the only strain of wheat was "Turkey Red," which was hardy enough for our climate, smut-resistant, and a good yielder. But my father and his friends never tired of exchanging horror stories about an earlier strain known as "Galgalis," which yielded bumper crops but produced a chaff so poisonously itchy that itinerant sack-sewers avoided fields of it like the plague, and hardy Missouri-bred farmers thought it no disgrace to come in and take showers or baths at noon! True to form, the Ramseys were among the last to give it up. ...

Farming was then not without its skills and tensions, but it was hardly agribusiness or the physically and economically frantic enterprise it became when irrigation arrived in the late 1940s. Horses, threshing machines, and wagons gave way to tractors, trucks, and combines in the 1920s, much to the relief of my father, who had wrangled, harnessed, and fed and watered enough horseflesh, he said, to operate the U.S. Cavalry for a month of Sundays. Nonetheless he sentimentally kept two old pensioners, Dix and Bess, for occasional haying and rock-hauling duties until they died of old age in my time.

What you did to be a wheat farmer was, first, in early spring to look out your upstairs window for color in your fields, the most delicately beautiful green in the vegetable rainbow; it would appear overnight, in late March or early April. Then you prayed for spring rains which, if they came, also brought on a fine crop of weeds on the summer fallow— Chinese lettuce, lamb's-quarter, mullein, several kinds of mustard, and the ubiqitous cheatgrass. So, not long after you finished plowing last year's stubble, you ventured out with your rod-weeder, which dragged an old spiketooth or springtooth harrow behind it to break up the clods if possible. Clods in bad years could become as big and dense as paving stones.

If I never have happier solitude than I've had in the seat of an old John Deere Model "G," weeding in late spring on the rim, I'll not complain, dear Lord—the hypnotically regular twin-cylinder detonations of the tractor, to which songs could be shouted or even poems hollered with pleasing effect; the clear light, as yet without summer glare and dazzle; winter snow on the mountains still, but green on the foothills; the sense of power awakening in the earth and in me, rolling over it in third or fourth gear, the buried rod of the weeder roiling the moist soil and pulling up weeds as deftly as a florist's hand, while we charged clockwise around the field of last year's harvest, spiralling inward until, at last, on the fourth day, we reached the invisible mysterious center of the land and finished. Then we would do it all over again, perhaps with a spring-tooth weeder, in a month or so. But I digress.

Through June and July, as the crop grew, and began to "turn," there wasn't much to do with it, except for after-dinner excursions into the fields to see how the wheat was "stooling." As many as twenty or more stalks with heads could "stool" out from one planted kernel, and this was the basis of bumper crops. And in the horizontal light just before sunset, we could see to "rogue" the tall rye-grass that always sprouted in the crop and could take over a field in a few years if not attended to.

By the end of July, when afternoon temperatures rose to ninety and big thunderheads began to float up out of the southwest like ghost ships, you got ready for the one critical episode of the year, the Main Event—harvest. The big ungainly grasshopper-like combines—John Deeres, Internationals, Holts, and Olivers—were pulled out of their sheds, reassembled, and groomed; harvest help was signed up off the street, or in the tavern, or sometimes out of the hobo jungle behind the depot. For once in the simple year, with everything riding on the harvesting of one crop, life became urgent, agitated, combat-like, heroic. People yelled at each other; mistakes were dealt with summarily and without quarter. Life revolved around the roaring, pulsing, inhumanly dusty combines—factories on wheels—and around the hard coppery grain that somehow gushed out of their innards. The big Bemis and Chase wheat sacks, like cartoon money-bags, were jigged full, artfully sewn up from ear to ear by the sack-sewer, ignominiously dumped into the stubble in bunches of seven or eight, and trucked off to the depot, day after day through August, field after field. My mother served up huge meals for the crew noon and evening; sometimes, in the hottest weather, she angelically took out lemonade at midafternoon, when we were shut down for "greezin" or repairs.

This was the season when we *lived* one of my father's maxims: "Never get in the way of someone at his work." This meant not talking silly on the job, or asking tomfool questions, or having to be told something twice, or succumbing (as I often did) to a mysterious form of distraction known to my family as lollygagging. In my father's world, the kind of person most likely to get in the way of one's work was a city dweller, and I grew up believing that cities, even little burgs like Madras, were teeming with triflers and lollygaggers.

One afternoon, late in what had proved to be a difficult harvest, as we were just opening a field and therefore still close to the road, a man arrived in a shiny car. He got out, carrying a briefcase, and walked a few feet towards the lurching combine. He lifted his hand, a gesture half wave of greeting and half signal to stop. Oh-oh, I thought. My father nodded curtly from the tractor—and opened the throttle. Forty-five minutes later as we came round again, the man was still there, standing forlornly in the stubble, now minus his briefcase. I was afraid that he might be foolish enough to try to stand his ground in front of the Caterpillar, but instead he scrambled in from the side. My father acknowledged his submission by slowing down slightly; as soon as the man was perched unsteadily on the draw-bar behind the tractor seat, however, he resumed full speed ahead (at a moderate walk). It was an insurance salesman, and when he jumped off after a full round of shouting in my father's ear, his blue suit was golden with chaff. He didn't look back, poor man, probably not all the way over the mountains to his office in Portland.

Breakdowns in harvest were inevitable given the pace, the rough ground, and the likelihood, in dry years of short stubble, of "harvesting" rocks. When they came, breakdowns dissipated some of the tensions in the field, for us kids at least, if not for our elders. On any afternoon, I could look from my perch on the "doghouse" of our combine and see which neighbors were broken down—no dust, a stopped combine, several pickups nosed in around it. You got so you could *hear* a breakdown about to occur; out of the normal roar and clatter, an odd syncopating thump or screech would appear. Then, generally before anybody could throw the main clutch out, it would grow into a terrible self-devouring clangor and the combine motor would stall. Silence, a whole field of it, broken only by my father's disgusted *"Shit!"* as he climbed off the tractor.

It could be a snapped draper belt or slat, or a broken elevator chain, or a bent sickle guide, or—worst of fates—a piece of rimrock through the cylinder, the whirling winnowing adjustable heart of the whole enterprise. *That* might take most of the day to uncover, and a day to repair, all in fiendishly awkward and knuckle-busting confines in the bowels of the machine—if indeed the local John Deere dealer had the parts you needed in stock, or could get them from Portland or The Dalles. Sometimes, carrying on a fine old American industrial tradition that must go back to Remington and Eli Whitney, the delivered parts wouldn't fit.

The most spectacular breakdown I remember was a main wheel breaking off our Oliver, pitching the whole machine over at a crazy angle, with me hanging on for dear life, and, another time, on my grandfather Mendenhall's antique Holt "hillside" machine, the twenty-foot counterbalanced wooden header boom snapping off, plunging the mighty header into the ground and catapulting me, the boy header-tender, ten feet into the air.

At least once I contributed directly to a breakdown. When I wasn't tending header, my usual job was the idiot-level task of pulling a rope every two minutes or so to dump the straw that accumulated in the straw-collector at the end of the combine. It was not exactly a job you could give yourself to, body, mind, and soul; and I would try to read, between jerks on the rope. One very hot afternoon the text was Plato's *Republic*, the Allegory of the Cave (Jowett's translation). I was simply transported out of the noise, the heat and chaff, the flying ants on my neck, and into the cool realm of Platonic forms—neglecting to pull my rope until the straw-walkers overloaded and a sprocket-chain broke. My dad was surprisingly forgiving—evidently this was lollygagging on a level beyond his experience. I went on reading through that harvest, but turned next to Dante's *Inferno* (Ciardi's translation), which worked out to be approximately twelve straw-dumps per canto.

Finally, unexpectedly to my hopeless young mind, we would be swathing down one final strip of wheat in the middle of the last field. Quite suddenly, then, everything was stubble, and harvest was over. Time to cheer and toss our filthy straw hats into the header behind the last stalks of wheat. This ceremony my brother and I learned from an old sack-sewer; our father was never so demonstrative. He would already be calculating the yield, from the wheat-haulers' tare-weight receipts at the depot. Twenty-five bushels per acre was a very good high average; and only once in what proved to be the last big year for dryland farming in these parts, 1948, did we hit forty bushels. Ours were piker yields compared to what Umatilla and Palouse farmers got every year with far less trouble, but then they didn't have our scenery.

Harvest done, we turned to the next enterprise, hauling straw out of the now cancelled fields. Two good compatible forkmen could pitch several acres of the big straw-dumps an hour, as the truck started and stopped, crawling between the long rows of dumps, always on the downwind side, and the "tromper" up on the load reeled and staggered, trying to make each trip to the straw stack worthwhile. At age nine I learned how to drive, after a fashion, pressed into service behind the wheel of an old Ford truck with a jackrabbit clutch. First I threw the tromper, my brother, clear off the load with one of my wild starts; then in desperation I discovered that I could leave the truck in gear and secretly ride the clutch, then *ease* it out and coax the truck into motion. In two hours, of course, I had developed a severe case of jitters and burnt the clutch out.

It may have been the same year, hauling straw one morning off a field south of our house, that Dad and one of my cousins killed seven sleeping rattlesnakes under seven consecutive dumps. After my brother had gamely tromped the straw into a load and they began to pitch it onto the stack, they discovered two more rattlers in the truck, by now no longer sleepy.

My father, never one to risk much time or money on the ingenious labor-saving devices that tempted other farmers, did install unloading derricks at our two main stackyards. The truckloads were pitched on top of rope or cable nets, and then at the stackyards these nets, bulging with several tons of straw, were supposed to be drawn up out of the truck, positioned over the stack, and then dropped. This dramatic operation was peformed by the man "building" the stack, who yanked on a trigger rope dangling beneath the load swaying over his head, and ran like hell as the straw tumbled down. Sometimes he didn't run fast or far enough, or stumbled, and we had to dig him out; sometimes he triggered the load prematurely, and it fell in the wrong place, or over the side. Occasionally the net rigging would foul or break, and the whole load would dangle in the air like a threat, or it would trip itself and fall back in the truck or onto the ground, to be pitched angrily and with twice the difficulty back onto the stack. My bachelor uncle Max, who was often a bemused participant in these labors, once tried to console my father after such a mishap: "Well, anyhow, Gus, it sure was spectacular!"

As I write this, I realize that one of the reasons I love the writings of William Faulkner is that, beyond any other writer, he knows and conveys the essential comic violence of farm life, as in that great Flem Snopes story, "Spotted Horses." Faulkner helps me remember, from my farmboy days, the wonderful violence of large animals and of crude and unwieldy farm machines—and the often drastic behavior of men and women trying to manage either or both. My father was often an irascible and always an accident-prone man, who once broke his foot merely kicking the rump of a stubborn shoat-pig to make it go up a loading-chute. A degree of overt violence was universal in our lives, I think, beginning with the brutal extremes of the climate. But I remember it, despite the very real element of physical danger and fear, as often being very funny.

Rarely, thank God, did people go after each other physically, but language, generally flat and laconic amongst us, could rise to wonderful heights of magical abuse, and actions sometimes spoke more eloquently of exasperation than words. Once my father's dear cowboy friend Lloyd, a gentle and churchly man of Baptist persuasion, came upon me trying to get a balky pack mule to move (we were on a pack-trip around Mt. Jefferson). Its hooves were planted in the trail like plowshares. Lloyd, who was never heard to swear even mildly but who knew mules, tried a few whistles and chirps and Indian noises, tried his quirt, tried a pine-branch—and then removed a short length of chain from the mule's pack, and began to belabor the beast over its tail, all the while whistling "Onward Christian Soldiers" breathlessly, whanging out each triumphant note with the chain on the mule's rump. That mule marched all day like a good Christian.

But I was talking about straw-hauling after harvest. The great incentive to finish with the straw was that we could then take a vacation, generally a camping trip up in the Cascade forests, far from combines and chaff and straw piles. One afternoon in August 1945, as we were topping out one of the main stacks in front of our house, we heard the Warm Springs mill whistle hoot over and over again. Presently an endless line of cars appeared on the highway, heading for town, horns blaring. Somebody who knew us leaned out of his window and hollered "THE WAR'S OVER—JAPS SURRENDERED—BIG SHINDIG IN TOWN TONIGHT!" We actually quit early, an unheard-of concession. I remember reflecting that if this had happened during harvest, we wouldn't have paid any attention, and a few days later we would have been up in the mountains. Excellent timing, General McArthur!

That night, we gathered in the Madras City Park to sing patriotic songs and hymns; the soldiers from the airbase north of town had hoisted a piano onto a flatbed truck and then lifted my mother up to play on it. Hoarded prewar booze was passed around, scandalously, in full view of the Methodist and Christian churches. Before the celebration divided between the revelers and the sobersides, talk ran through the crowd of the newfangled bombs—just two of them—that had destroyed the two Japanese cities. Somebody joked about getting such a device war-surplus to blow the rocks, once and for all, out of his back forty. But in church that Sunday, our stern preacher asked the question that still haunts our lives, mushroom-shaped. "The terrible war is over, thank God," she said, "but consider, what new violence have we begun?"

But in that tumultuous year, as always, life did resume its simple rounds. After a week or so of camping, we came back home to perform the last laborious sacraments of dryland farming: burning what was left of the straw piles, carrying the burning straw in iron pitchforks from pile to pile until the whole field crackled and smothered in sweet white smoke; weeding and harrowing the fallow ground if need be; drilling next year's crop; and—a special local version of Farmer Adam's Curse—hauling rocks.

It is early November, the first snow is on the mountains, and I am too young yet to go to school. My dad has hitched old Dix and Bess to a stoneboat, and we have gone out on the rim to resume the farmer's perpetual war against the encroaching stony ballast of the land. Rocks of every size, shape, and color seemed to boil up each year out of some inexhaustible petrous nursery below to wear out plowshares, snag weeder-rods, and rattle through a combine's delicate innards like cannonballs. The south side of the field is bracketed with a double row of rocks chest high and four feet wide, a monument to the fortitude (and hernias) of our predecessors. But for me it is a fine game to tramp afield with my dad this morning, heft a good rock in each hand like a caveman, carry them back to the stoneboat, and lob them in, as he does.

Half an hour later, it is not so fine a game, and after an hour, I ask him why we are doing this anyway. He says, jesting, "Because the rocks don't look good in a field," and he invites me to build a little rock cairn so that we can see what ground we've covered. I am intrigued and set to work, as he goes on with the stoneboat. I learn much there about gravity, and balance, and the intransigence of irregular objects, and when he comes back, I have made us a man out of piled-up rocks, a man of many grating and unstable parts, standing up in the field, much like those wonderful arctic landmarks the Inuit call *inuksuk*. My father admires my stone man, and then, before I can protest, dismantles him into the stoneboat. I squall, and he says, "Well, then make another one, to mark this next row." And so I do, all day long across the field, making stone men to praise our work and assert our image.

❧

THESE WERE, ROUGHLY, THE SEASONS OF OUR FARMING each year, until the coming of irrigation. They were what it was given to us to do with our land, seemingly as fixed and irrevocable as the passage of winter into spring, and spring into summer and fall. Everything else—unseasonable weather, illness, injury, arrivals and departures, birth and death—seemed somehow incidental to the order of our accustomed work.

But soon after the end of the war, my father did impose another order on the year, secondary to the farming and less complicated, but at times just as demanding. From his boyhood on, he'd wanted to be a stockman: no doubt this seemed to him like an appropriate second-generation fulfillment of the western dream that had impelled his father to leave Missouri for Oregon in the first place. He'd kept good horses and a few Herefords for a number of years, affecting the style of a rancher more than most of his family and neighbors. But in 1946 he startled everybody by buying a rundown fourteen hundred-acre sheep ranch, a good hour's rough drive to the east, in the foothills of the Ochoco Mountains.

This place, which my mother named the "Sky Ranch" after the Sierra retreat of the Barber Family on radio, seemed to be in a different world than the "home place" on Agency Plains. It was high—overfour thousand feet, much of it—and hilly, sloping up to the east; the lower reaches were all juniper and sagebrush, giving way to pockets of Ponderosa pine and Douglas fir higher up. It had its own weather and was wet, at least by Agency Plains standards, with springs and creeks everywhere. It was remote and wild country, and haunted; after twenty years or so of intensive homesteading (if subsistence farming can be called "intensive") all but a few of its homesteaders had simply walked away in the 1920s, God knows where, leaving the shacks and yards of their brief purpose strewn in nearly every draw and meadow. By the time we bought it, the Sky Ranch included the claims of at least nine "entrymen," as homesteaders were designated—all gone now. Deer and even elk grazed around our old farmhouse, coyotes skulked along the roads, and the fields, tiny and irregular by our lowland standards, were already reverting to nature. It was and is a place of immediate and inexhaustible wonder, a country so peaceful, so far removed in time and space from the great world's cares and alarums that, as our friend William Stafford once wrote of it, "You can walk all day there and look back" ("Finding Sky Ranch").

The first year, we plowed the fields up—the soil black as coal—and planted a mixture of wheat and crested wheat-grass. The wheat was to serve as a harvestable cover crop for the grass, which would, once established, provide summer pasture for our future herd. It was an unusually rainy year. The wheat grew so tall that a grown man could walk into a field and disappear in green (small boys were afraid to), and some of it never did ripen. According to Dad's master plan, this was the only time we tried to crop the place, but the wheat-grass established itself abundantly, and we were ready to go into the cow-and-calf business in earnest. Before long we'd built up a herd of seventy-five to eighty Hereford cows and a few bulls—not registered breeding stock, but good solid animals.

The cowboy side of the year went something like this. In early spring, the cows would start calving in the feedlots in front of our house at the home place. Feeding them hay and straw morning and night, we kept an eye out for trouble, especially with the heifers. Sometimes we had to assist at breech births, and my mother thought nothing of boarding one or more half-frozen whiteface babies on the back porch, until they were able to stand up and nurse. Once we actually skinned a dead newborn calf and tied the hide on a poor little waif that had been abandoned by its mother. The bloody disguise kept sliding off, but it worked: within a day or two the waif and the bereaved cow were inseparably cow-and-calf. By the time the ground had thawed out and yellowbells were in bloom, the feedlots would be alive with gangs of long-legged silly calves, all running and bucking in concert, tails in the air, as if possessed by the contrary winds of spring.

Good thing they didn't know what was coming. Generally in May, when the winds had subsided and the ground was safely dry, we rounded them up for branding. Our brand, of which I was inordinately proud, was a very old design out of the Oregon High Desert, "Box Dot" on the left rib, so: ⊡ . If you hit just the right place on the calf's side, the brand would stretch equilaterally around the dot as the critter grew, until it looked at maturity like a square signboard two feet across, with a cryptic dot in the center. We generally had outside help from Lloyd Luelling and others, at whose brandings we would in turn assist. The corral became a sort of gothic assembly line; somebody roping each calf, another catching its legs and throwing it down, a third tending the branding iron in the fire and giving vaccinations against blackleg and other dread diseases, a fourth, armed with a sharp knife, managing the earmarks (a notch over the left ear and one under the right) and castrating the poor bull calves.

This last operation always gave me the wimwams, although in truth it seemed to hurt the young calves less than the earmarking and branding. Such an arbitrary meddling with destiny! We never dined on "Rocky Mountain oysters" in our household, but once on a neighbor's ranch, I watched the mother and daughters gathering them out of the bloody dirt with a peculiar glee than cost me my appetite that noon.

Then, in late spring, with the grass well established at the Sky Ranch, came the move to summer pasture. Sometimes in company with neighbors and their herds, but more often alone, we simply rounded up the herd and started off cross-country to the east. Like in the old days; like in the movies! Barring some serious misadventure, our drives took two nights and parts of three days. (A paltry drive, compared to my great-uncle Walt McCoin's yearly drive up to Sparks Lake in the High Cascades, which usually took over a week.) After a trip or two each way, the herd established its traveling leadership. Two or three veteran cows would fight between themselves for pride of place in front, but together they led the whole dusty, bawling, unstable herd like prophets. The trouble generally came in the rear echelons. Calves stupidly would get inside fences, to straggle alongside the herd for miles; bulls would break out of the herd to fight other bulls at farms we were passing; on country roads, some impatient SOB out for a drive would try to force his car through the herd and spook it.

I remember three serious stampedes, each occurring on the drive home from Sky Ranch in November, when dark skies and cold winds seemed to dispose the cows to spook easily. One ruckus came when we imprudently tried to force the herd right through the north end of Madras, and the lead cows balked at the freshly painted yellow lines on the streets, thinking them cattle-guards. Another happened as we trailed past an abandoned homestead, and an old windmill suddenly began to tear itself to pieces in the high winds. A third stampede—the worst— occurred when the first *Oregon Journal* helicopter discovered us and choppered right down to eyebrow level for some feature-page photography, scattering terrified cows and horses in every direction. It took hours to regroup after that one. Unmollified by a handsome aerial photo of the fracas in the *Journal,* my father muttered darkly about carrying a shotgun. …

The much more common problem was sheer dusty boredom and exasperation from trying to urge a herd of lazy cows and skittish calves to walk thirty miles, browsing along the way but not stopping, while staying out of fields and going through the right gates. The first day out we all had brave cries and catcalls to make them go; the next day, hoarse from yelling in the dust, I usually resorted to rattling a pebble in a tin can or slapping my Levis. The strain of maintaining and guiding brute inertia wore us down fast. I would dream of plodding hooves and dust and bellering for a week afterward, and I would be sore for days from unconsciously urging everything along from the saddle.

In truth, although my father became a successful stockman who knew his herd by heart and was always in control of it, and my brother grew up as an expert horseman, I was no cowboy and I knew it. I was on reasonably good terms with our horses, Flicka, Dolly, Blue, Traveler, and Sky, but to me riding generally meant hard work and long hours, divided about equally between boredom and fear. None of my best friends were cowboys, either. I saw sure-footed Flicka slip and fall on my brother and break his leg as they were chasing a cow on the highway; I saw my father's tall horse Traveler step in a badger's hole at full gallop during a Sky Ranch roundup and cartwheel on and over him, breaking his leg in thirteen places. I had my own share of minor horseback accidents and decided early on that, for thrills, I'd stick to machines. On my twelfth Christmas, in place of the young horse I should have wanted, my folks conceded and gave me a motor scooter.

The only times I truly relished my periodic service as reluctant cowpoke were when we were trailing the herd around Madras, or even through it. Then the boredom and tensions of the job were offset by the prospect of being seen and wondered at by townspeople and schoolmates, as we nudged the critters of the Box-Dot down side streets and across vacant lots. Then, full of the romance of it all, I sat very tall in the saddle. Once when I was about thirteen, I nearly ran down a man and his son on the sidewalk in front of the post office, as my horse scrambled to bring a steer back into line. Far from being upset, the man told his little boy, "Look closely there, son, you're seeing a little bit of the real Old West!" And over my shoulder, insufferably, I said, "That's right, son."

As time went on, it grew more and more difficult to trail the herd to summer range and back. Around Madras suburbs sprang up on our routes, while out in the country irrigated farmers were tearing down the tight five-wire fences that the old farmers had used, replacing them—if at all—with puny electric fences. We would soon start *trucking* the herd to pasture and back, a grueling two-day job each way that was much harder on men and cows than the drives. But there was one last memorable adventure before that part of our Old West faded away.

We were bringing home the cows: it was unseasonably hot for November. As we neared the eastern outskirts of Madras, my father cautioned us drovers about keeping the herd especially tight, because of the new houses and yards on our route. In particular, he said, watch out for open gates and doors. I was riding a rear point when suddenly I saw a heifer break off from the main herd, followed by a couple of steers, heading for the open back door of a new bungalow. I spurred to catch up and yelled, which only served to speed up the action. As if running on rails, the heifer galloped up to the door and right through it, with the steers close behind.

Uncertain what to do now, I went around to the front door and waited discreetly. After what seemed like an eternity, I heard terrible noises from inside and then the heifer exploded through the screen door, something lacy caught on her horns, and skidded across the porch. She was closely followed, in eerie silence, by the lady of the house, with the steers right at her heels. The critters headed back toward the herd; I thought it impolitic to wait around for future developments, and got the hell out of there myself. I don't think my father ever knew what happened, but that was the last Box-Dot old-style Wild West cattle drive through Madras. I reckon there's an ordinance against such things now.

❖

AND THEN, CORRESPONDING TO THE SEASONS of the year when we left the wheatfields to themselves, there was school. In my father's boyhood, with homesteads on every quarter-section, there were several one-room schools on and around the Plains. But by the time my brother and I started, there was just one, located opposite Hi Links' house on the north end, auspiciously known as "New Era School, No. 35." It was about three miles up the graveled Market Road from our place; we were driven to it, or rode horseback, or bicycled.

The school sat back east of the road; it was a fine big squarish building, actually painted (white), with a porch on the southwest corner where the teacher stood and rang her handbell to call us in. Inside, there was a cloakroom leading through two doors to the big airy single classroom, with tall windows on the east and north sides, and blackboards on the west. Behind a curtain in the southeast corner of the room was a cozy library with books to the ceiling—an irresistible and magical place. The teacher's big oak desk faced ours; we sat in four rows, very loosely ranked by age and size. I don't recall less than twelve pupils or more than twenty-one; usually there was at least one from each grade, but little attention was paid to grade levels *per se.*

A huge old Waterbury stove sat in the back, with an iron shield and railing around it, good for drying mittens and caps in winter, and if you pressed crayons against the hot metal, they would bubble and run down in interesting streaks of oily color. There was no electricity, of course, no indoor plumbing, and no audiovisual aids, except for an old donated Victrola, on which we played huge Music Appreciation records featuring the "Longines Symphonette," and sometimes, at noon, my brother's precious Harry James boogie-woogie records.

Here again I seem to have been bred more for the nineteenth century than for the twentieth, but there are worse anachronisms, maybe. I know enough horror stories about one-room country schools to appreciate how lucky we were for teachers. My first (a pedagogical saint if there ever was one) was Mrs. Elva G. Hall, who as a young woman had taught my father at another school and later had taught college English. Now in her late sixties, widowed and unwell, Mrs. Hall was back where she had begun her career, in a one-room school in central Oregon teaching roughnecks, because the war had dispersed all the younger teachers.

Mrs. Hall lived in the little teacherage south of the school, and in my first year the school board built a wooden walk between the two buildings so that she could avoid the mud and snow. Alas, the boards iced over in January, and she fell and broke some ribs. My Aunt Lela came in as a substitute for a few weeks, putting my brother and me on the spot. We were also on the spot with my father's half-sister, Aunt Lillian Watts, who was Jefferson County's first school superintendent and remained in the job until her retirement in the late 1950s; fortunately, she only visited school in the spring to administer the county-wide achievement tests, and we tried to play like she wasn't kin, lest she fuss over us.

We all mythify, I think, our first-grade teachers; no doubt it has something to do with the fact that they are the ones to unleash in us the awesome powers of written language and numbers. I thought that Mrs. Hall was in reality two witches: a good morning witch, clear-eyed, alert, and cheerful; and a bad afternoon witch, cranky, red-faced, wheezing, and much older. The pathetic fact was that she was suffering from hardening of the arteries and hypertension, which probably meant that after lunch and a nap, she felt miserable all afternoon. Soon after she retired and went to live with her son in Denver, she wrote to each of "her children" to tell us that she'd gone blind. Still she wrote us long wonderful letters, full of flattering questions about ourselves, her unguided script wavering bravely across the page. She was the first person I loved who died.

There was a certain imbalance in Mrs. Hall's teaching. She burned like a filament whenever we passed in our lessons through the realms of language, literature, history, and art; our forays into arithmetic and science were likely to be perfunctory, tentative,and brief. Or am I only remembering my own early affinities? Well, her school proved to be no nursery for mathematicians, or physicists, or businessmen; I remain a booby at anything beyond simple math. But often when I am working on a poem, or reading one, she is there somehow, in her good-witch guise, plump in one of her shapeless shiny brown dresses with a brooch at her neck, cheerfully urging me to claim yet more of the dictionary's gift of fine words.

When she had gone through the lessons our various grade levels demanded, she would read to us, at length and with great feeling. Never mind that her texts were of the order of *The Little Lame Prince* and *Toby Tyler, or Six Weeks with the Circus* and the poetry of Arthur Guiterman and Eleanor Farjeon; never mind that an outsider might have found it strange that she often wept over such matter. Because we loved her, we wept too; it seemed the least we could do. Between our preacher's urgent praying, my father's swearing, and Mrs. Hall's reading out loud with tears, language was becoming strong stuff.

I used to ask cheekily whether the "new era" of our school had a name, and when it would grow into an old era. Mrs. Hall would smile indulgently and tell us that *we* were supposed to be the new era; I guess we believed her. But we were aware, too, that beyond the mountains and over the ocean, men who'd once sat at our desks and carved their initials on them were on jungly islands shooting and being shot at by the Japanese. We secretly hoped that before winning the war, the American forces would let themselves be pushed back as far as the Pacific states; we prepared ourselves accordingly.

By 1942 the Army airbase at the southern end of the Plains on what had been the Sam Mitchell homestead was in full operation; hotshot pilots were wringing out experimental fighter-planes, and using our broken landscape, it was rumored, to train for secret missions overseas. B-17 bombers were always zooming out of our canyons at treetop heights, pushing incredible waves of echoed sound before them. Once, two "Flying Fortresses" collided in formation over the Mutton Mountains north of the Plains and straggled right over our house, spewing flames and debris and parachutes. And one day after school, my dad and I watched an experimental clipped-wing Bell P-63 "King Cobra" powerdive thirty thousand feet into a plowed field just east of the school. The plane made a crater as deep and wide as a basement; the pilot, whose parachute didn't open, made his own crater a hundred yards away. We kids fancied that such important operations would surely draw the invaders our way; when a Japanese submarine shelled the Oregon coast in 1942, we assumed that the invasion of Agency Plains was imminent, and that we would soon become guerilla fighters, like the ones we were hearing about in the Philippines.

This collective fantasy, coupled with Mrs. Hall's utter indifference to formal recreation for her pupils, meant that we almost never played real games at noon or recess or before school, least of all games joining both sexes. No, we boys were digging in for battle. I think my brother Jimmie and his friend Gordon and some other kids started it in the summer of 1942. Beginning a half mile down the canyon below our house, they built a sequence of rimrock fortresses and lookout stations, in case the invaders came that way. It was agreed that we would make our last stand against General Tojo and his hordes, if it came to that, at New Era School.

That fall, what had begun as a little experimental foxhole in the loose dirt next to the road in front of school became a fine deep pillbox big enough to hold everybody—all the boys, that is. With childish singleness of purpose, we soon roofed it, camouflaged the roof with sod, and installed a periscope and a tin-can stove, brought in our toy guns and some foodstuffs, and became a military brotherhood, a guerilla band known as the "Red Moles." Gordon, who was artistic and clever, painted the flag. We had time, and mind, for nothing else.

The girls, feeling understandably jealous and neglected, mocked us and mounted one or two attacks, which were easily driven off with clods and verbal abuse. Poor things, they retreated to mope around the school building and murmur threats about telling Mrs. Hall. For a week or so they tried to imitate our enterprise under a flag proclaiming themselves the "Red Ants," but without a fortress or hideout there was no romance in it; soon they returned to dolls and tag, and even took up our forsaken game of snaring sagerats with string nooses.

Meanwhile, the grand excavations continued. The soil, unusually deep and loamy for the Plains, was irresistible for digging—dark, compact, lacking in rocks, and fragrant. First we tunnelled to the north about twenty feet, ending in a blind chamber; then we dug side tunnels, storage rooms, and an escape tunnel under the fence and into the borrow pit by the road. At home our parents were missing spades, trowels, and buckets; although we tried to wash away the evidence of our labors every day, our mothers were mystified by the chronic filthiness of our clothes and bodies. It was wonderful. Gordon and Jimmie dug a special sideroom, which they declared off-limits to us little kids; cigarettes and pin-up photos were suspected. No matter that I never learned to swing a baseball bat properly, or play jacks, or hopscotch, or marbles; it was enough to belong to the Red Moles, eating jelly sandwiches like K-rations in our candlelit earthworks, with someone on duty at the periscope, ready for all enemies!

In truth our enemies were all strangers. Our sociology, based on *fewness*, precluded playing war games in two or more opposing gangs, as children normally do; we wouldn't have thought of such formal playground warfare. And if the shunned girls had demanded admission with the magic words "We *really* mean it!" it would have been granted, not out of charity but to avoid strife. I think we feared internal strife more than anything. In my five years at New Era, I do not recall a single fight or feud, or even a good name-calling argument at school. There were occasional punitive "dirty tricks," when after repeated warnings we took steps to correct various bad habits in our schoolmates, like tattling or trying to be "bossy." Some of these measures were pretty drastic, but the tattling or bossing generally did stop as a consequence, the offender/victim forgave and was forgiven, and we carried on together as before.

As I conjure up my childhood there, growing up with my tiny circle of playmates, which was everybody else's circle, I marvel at the sheer repressive tranquility of it all. Given the ways of the world at large, I'm not sure that it was good training in how to live, or even psychologically healthy. But we did manage to get along, less than siblings and somehow more than friends. Snooping in my brother's "SECRET DIARY," as I tried to do at least once a month, I came upon this entry, which struck me as remarkable even then. "Friday. Today I *almost* got mad at Gordon. …"

Finally change invaded the Plains: the war ended, Gordon and Jimmie graduated and went to high school in town; Mrs. Hall retired; and in the fall of 1945 a new teacher arrived to take her place. Mrs. Hering was young—my parents' age: in fact she and my father had been high-school sweeties. She was, I already knew, red haired and high spirited. Any hopes we had of carrying on as the postwar Red Moles, perhaps in league with the United Nations, were dashed the first morning of school that September. "Well, boys," Mrs. Hering announced brightly, "that was quite an underground fort you had out by the road. When I came by last month to look the school over, I fell through the tunnels and sprained my ankle. No more of that, boys. The war's over, but we'll have team sports instead!"

So we filled in our beloved tunnels and brooded on rebellion. By the end of the second week, we'd secretly excavated a new, bigger, and better pillbox in a different corner of the schoolground; she found *that* even before we could roof it, and thanked us for digging such a fine big trashpit. We conceded defeat, returned our parents' long-lost digging tools, and resigned ourselves to learning the sissy sports of softball, soccer, and broom hockey.

So began the last new era of New Era School. Enrollment swelled, as whole neighborhoods from western Idaho moved to the Plains in advance of the opening of the North Unit Irrigation Project. Mrs. Hering, master teacher that she was, kept us hopping. One of us paid her the ultimate grudging tribute: "Good God, she sees everything!" At the furthest extreme from the furtive pleasures of the Red Moles campaign, she engineered an elaborate all-school musical pageant celebrating the Oregon Trail, with a red-cellophane campfire on stage and a life-sized replica of a prairie schooner painted "Oregon or Bust," around which we rallied to sing "Old Dan Tucker" and "Sourwood Mountain" while on the trail, and the Oregon state anthem, "Land of the Empire Builders," once we had reached the promised land.

Let no historian mock my fancy that with this childish pageant, our odd local extension of the Oregon Trail came to an end. We had done what we could with what was left of the frontier. Now the dryland fields were being leveled and subdivided and ditched for irrigation; rock-infested ground through which our grandfathers first drove a plow for free was selling for hundreds of dollars an acre. Outlanders who wore rubber boots and talked mysteriously about "headgates" and "subbing" and "ladino clover" were buying up the land and renaming one of our old market roads "Boise Drive."

People began to talk about a plan to consolidate New Era School with the Madras school system. Our parents fought it angrily, knowing that our little community, like many another, would lose its traditional center if the school closed. But when it came to a vote, the newcomers, who claimed to speak for the future in all things, won overwhelmingly. We would all go to town next fall, riding buses, to become "new kids" among strangers.

Near the end of school that last spring at New Era, the principal from Madras paid our teacher a call. Mrs. Hering had once taught under him, and she had confided to us that they were bitter enemies. It looked like he'd come out to rub salt in our wounds. It was afternoon recess, and he strutted right through our softball game "like a German general," someone whispered. Mrs. Hering met him on the porch, blocking his entrance. What she said to him, glaring down on his crewcut Prussian head, we couldn't hear, but her hands were making fists and her red hair was tossing. Suddenly he turned and began to stalk back to his car. Mrs. Hering covered her face with her hands. We followed him silently through the yard, and as he drove off, we all threw rocks and gravel at his car until it was out of range, on the way back to town.

OH MEMORY, MEMORY, to look into the upstairs dark and see the scattered homestead lights of Agency Plains again, the lights I once thought permanent as stars! And if I could, I'd go down to the phone in the kitchen, and ring five *longs*, the never-used Emergency Number, and say to all my listeners and rubberers, "Hello, this is Jerry, I have an emergency. Don't do anything different; just go on being yourselves in the old way as long as you can; but hear this. Our world here is going to change; the big world has surely found us out. We are about to fly apart from each other like sparks. I love you all; so long for now."

Two

THE FARM BOY, THE WIDOWED HOMESTEADER, AND THE OLD INDIAN: CONSERVING A STORY

❖❖

I HAVE BEEN HAUNTED BY A STORY for most of my life, since I first heard bits and pieces of it as a boy. In truth, it's not so much a story, as the *possibility* of one, hiding (or so I think) in a jumble of episodes, anecdotes, allusions, and conjectures, that has taken up room inside my head for many years, until the compulsion to find a narrative order in the stuff has overcome my skepticism about making anything of it.

Lest I seem in this endeavor to resemble the Ancient Mariner (or Joseph Conrad's narrator Marlow), forever condemned to seek the meaning of an experience by inflicting narrations of it on unwilling auditors, I should explain that the story I am searching for is strictly secondhand to me. Its events happened only to some people I knew, or knew about, and long before I was born. So my interests are not immediately personal ones, nor are they (so far as I can tell) aimed at expiation or vindication of anything or anyone. In trying to work out these interests, I will in effect be endeavoring to create a kind of *meta*-narrative, a story around a story, in which the outer narrative will, maybe, stabilize and consolidate and clarify the inner one.

Before proceeding further, I should offer what will be the first of several provisional formulations of the original tale. It belonged, during his life, to a man named John Campbell, of Madras, Oregon. He told episodes from it and frequently made allusions to it to me and others over many years, so that it came to occupy a certain collective imaginative space amongst his familiars; but he never wrote it down, nor is there any record of his ever having told the story as a complete unit, so that it is not only totally oral (and on a very limited basis of oral tradition at that), but unformulated, unrealized, embryonic. If there is a compost heap of oral traditions, this one would surely be a candidate for composting! But instead, let's try to reclaim and reconstitute it.

33

Stripped to its barest bones, the story would go like this:

> Once, around 1906, three men spent several weeks in late
> summer wandering on horseback along the Cascade
> Mountains in Oregon, between Mt. Jefferson and the
> South Sister. They were: a young unmarried rancher's son
> named John Campbell, a widower in his late thirties named
> Frank Stangland, and an older Wasco Indian named Jim
> Polk. Their intended destination was an alpine creek
> southwest of the mountain known as the South Sister
> where, according to Jim Polk, some of his people had once
> found gold nuggets; but just before the three reached the
> place, Jim Polk "spooked," having remembered another,
> sinister story about the location, and consequently refused
> to lead his friends to it. So they turned around and
> returned to the Warm Springs Indian Agency.

So much, then, for a provisional narrative peg from which to hang our enterprise. No sex, no violence, no heroic achievements or tragedies— in its apparently anticlimactic form, in fact, a kind of Shaggy Dog story. How to locate what we are proposing to do with such material, according to which academic domains and intellectual motives? In order to "identify" and conserve a story that never seems to have attained its full expressive form, in performance or otherwise, which specialists should we consult? The folklorists? The narratologists? Ethnohistorians? Literary theorists of many stripes? I confess I don't know; maybe all of the above, wherever help seems to be forthcoming, and maybe such uncertainty between intellectual domains is one good subversive reason to pursue the project in the first place!

Maybe the most sensible thing to do with such perplexing material would be to try to reinvent it as a short story, but that seems too simple, and I want to proceed on the assumption that the story *can* be reconstituted without recourse to fabulation or fictional inventions. What I want, no doubt impossibly, is the whole adventure as John Campbell might have told it, nothing left out, its scanty array of details identified and related as narrative facts, and contextualized as fully as possible through the exercise of whatever kind of research seems promising.

The term that the anthropologist Claude Lévi-Strauss uses to describe a characteristic mythic activity of Tricksters, *bricolage*, might aptly be applied to this project. *Bricolage* means a sort of "cobbling together" of a significant order out of "available materials," as performed by a *bricoleur* or handyman. So in Native American myth, Coyote or Raven sort of improvises the forms of reality, for better and for worse, as he wanders through a raw and unfinished, "unstoried" mythic world.[1] I have, I hope, no tricksterish motives, but the image of a handyman cobbling something together out of what's at hand is as good as any to describe what I want to do with the story of John Campbell, Frank Stangland, and Jim Polk.

How different, how much simpler the task would be, of course, if only they were alive to narrate the adventure, patiently answer our questions about it, and no doubt argue between themselves about what really happened in the mountains. But the fact that they can't do this, and that their story has virtually disappeared from all speech and memory, poses, I think, a special kind of obligation. Coming along behind them, inheriting pieces and shadows of what might be their story, we must do the best we can with what we've got; *and we must try.* I use the first person plural here, not as a rhetorical flourish, but to suggest that we are all potentially custodians and conservators of unwritten materials—stories, anecdotes, sayings, songs from family, jobs, local tradition, and elsewhere—material of such a nature that if *we* don't try to conserve it, knowing what we know, who will?

To undertake such work is crucial if we are going to maintain for ourselves and our inheritors an idea of "popular culture" in the Far West or anywhere that is more localized and more nourishing to the imagination than, say, *Seinfeld* or the *Guinness Book of Records.* To the stern Biblical question, "Who shall inherit the earth?" lovers of folklore and local history must add, and act upon, a related question, "And what stories will they inherit about *this* corner of the earth?"

There is, I believe, an ecology of memory, imagination, and story, just as there is an ecology of land, water, and air. Indeed, as the poet Gary Snyder has been saying for years, the two kinds of knowing and remembering are very closely related, and the moral imperatives of one are implied in those of the other. In Snyder's view, true conservation must involve the inner realms of the spirit and the imagination, as well as the outer realms of the biosphere.[2] Cultivating and conserving the apparently inexhaustible but often wasted resources of the human spirit may well help us to conserve the all-too-clearly limited and exhaustible resources of the world around, under, and above us.

1. Claude Levi-Strauss, "The Structural Study of Myth," in *Structural Anthropology*, transl. by Jacobsen and Schoepf (Garden City: Doubleday, 1967), pp. 250 ff.
2. See Snyder's "As for Poets," in *Turtle Island* (New York: New Directions, 1974), pp. 87-8; and his *The Practice of the Wild* (San Francisco: North Point, 1990).

In particular, as we work to conserve and understand the oral/traditional stories of Native Americans, we perceive that a crucial function of such stories has always been to help the people who knew and cherished them to maintain a proper imaginative relationship with the rest of the natural order. Native attitudes towards what we call "the environment" were clearly shaped from childhood on by *stories*—Coyote stories dramatizing the disastrous consequences of human greed and wastefulness of natural resources; hero stories showing the people the life-and-death importance of living in harmony with nature, participating with knowledge and reverence in its processes, rather than abusing or exploiting them.

Given our ecological predicaments now, and worse ones impending, such stories have much to tell us about our human obligations to the land we have appropriated from the Indians. In particular, the ecological emphasis in Native myths suggests that we need to find ways to *reimagine* our proper place in the natural order. Scientific understandings are indispensable to us, obviously, but it is clear that they are not enough to bring us and our culture into alignment, mind and spirit, with the American environment and its ecosystems. Hence the ecological importance of the work now underway to conserve traditional Native American literature; such work is itself a kind of mental ecology, and although we must find our own "post-modern" ways to engage the imagination in the cause of the environment, Native stories point out the need to do so, and the way.

But I want to make my case for an ecology of memory, imagination, and story on an even wider basis. At first glance, John Campbell's tale about how he and his companions didn't find gold one summer doesn't appear to carry with it much environmental significance, but conserving it seems no less important for that—simply because it is a *story*, after all, something once told, at least in pieces, and still tellable. As the wise man Uchendu declares in Chinua Achebe's novel *Things Fall Apart*, "There is no story that is not true."[3] Uchendu is reflecting in the 1870s on the impending disruption of Nigerian Ibo culture by British colonialists and missionaries, and what he means is that to survive in times of drastic change and upheaval, people need to pay attention to what they tell each other in story form: both traditional narratives, and hearsay tales of new wonders and dangers. The Native American writer Leslie Silko takes the same position at the beginning of her novel *Ceremony*: "You don't have

---

3. Chinua Achebe, *Things Fall Apart* (New York: Fawcett, 1969), p. 130.

anything if you don't have the stories./They are all we have, you see,/all we have to fight off/illness and death."[4] Silko means, of course, the traditional Pueblo myths that her protagonist Tayo must recover and re-imagine if he is to recover from his wartime traumas; but all through her wonderful novel runs the idea, surely relevant to Indians and Anglos alike, that as life itself is an ongoing story, so our human penchant for *storying* the truth of experience is literally a way of life, a gift of survival not to be trifled with, but cherished and conserved.

- "There is no story that is not true."
- "You don't have anything if you don't have the stories."
- Or, to mangle Shakespeare a little: "If all the world is sometimes like a stage, what happens in the world is *always* like a story."

Now I'm no raconteur, as my children used to remind me when I tried to play like one at bedtime, but I'm a good listener and I know some pretty good yarns, from Anglo and Native American repertories, and so the question might be asked, "Why single out a story as incomplete, as full of gaps and shadows as this one, in order to educe the value of an ecology of story?" Well, first of all, precisely because such gaps and shadows are what the kind of literary conservancy I am proposing ought to be able to rectify—so as a story, this one provides a good test case. But the question of why *this* story requires other answers, too.

One is simply that I may be the only living inheritor of this story who has any interest in preserving it. My friend John Campbell, who died in Madras in 1978, age ninety, was one of the indispensable pioneers of central Oregon, who in later years thought of himself as a dedicated oral historian rather than as a yarn-spinner; in fact he used to take sly delight in reducing the tall tales of pioneer life as told by some of his contemporaries to plain narratives of documentable fact. I can't know for sure what he would want me to do with the story, now that it is mine, except to keep it firmly anchored in factuality; but, as with most legacies material and spiritual, I am haunted by all the questions I was too incurious and unimaginative to ask him when I could have, and compelled now to try to answer them myself, as best I can.

From an interpretive standpoint, looking at the outline of the story as we have it, I see two possible configurations of meaning and value, one historical and one archetypal. The historical meaning lies in the fact that the narrated events take place in a time, very late in the history of the American West, when, in central Oregon, Indians and "white-eyes"

---

4. Leslie Silko, *Ceremony* (New York: New American Library, 1977), p. 2.

(as they sometimes call us) were still new to each other, still sorting each other out, still capable of interacting with a directness and unironic openness that would later become virtually impossible. In 1906 there were still people on the Warm Springs Reservation who could remember pre-Reservation life, and the old Wasco Chinookan and Warm Springs Sahaptin stories, and the languages in which they were embedded, continued to be elements of a still vital traditional Native culture, even though it had been "reservationized" for half a century.

On the other side (literally on the east side of the Deschutes River), in 1906 the sparse white homesteading population of the region looked to their Indian neighbors for seasonal farm help, for horses, for advice on everything from the local climate and trail finding to Native medicines, for entertainment (as at the grand Warm Springs Fourth of July celebrations), for friendship. As noted before, one of John Campbell's lifelong *tillikums*, a Wasco elder named Charlie Jackson, liked to tell about his father Jim's initial encounter with my grandfather Ramsey and his family, when they first arrived from Missouri and took up their homestead on the rim overlooking the Warm Springs Reservation, in 1902. Jim Jackson reported to his family that these newcomers seemed like good people, but added that "they don't know much of anything, here, and if they're going to make it they're going to need a lot of help." Such anecdotes, and John Campbell's tale itself, serve as useful reminders that there have been local moments of relatively easy, co-equal interaction and interdependence between Indians and whites, within the long mostly dismal history of their relations in the West.

The archetypal pattern in the story focuses on John Campbell himself. He was about eighteen that summer, old enough to declare his independence, at least for several weeks after harvest, from working on his father's ranch, old enough to undertake, with something of the confidence and savvy of a man, the perfect boyhood adventure of going into the mountains with an Indian guide in search of gold. Imagine the prospects! Shades of Jim Hawkins and Long John Silver, of Saxton Pope Jr. and Ishi, of Erskine Wood and Chief Joseph—such adventures of initiation and "coming out" appeal to us all with the force of archetype: we've been there ourselves, at least in our dreams. Every time John Campbell told me episodes from his mountain journey, fifty and sixty years later, he did so with a warmth and animation that suggested that he was tapping once again into what he counted to be the great formative adventure of his life.

But being in his own mind a historian, not a storyteller, he never once told me the whole adventure in one telling, nor did he do so to anyone else that I know of, not even his two sons. And on that problematic note, let's turn again to the story, and begin by retelling it, this time including all of its limited baggage of expressive details, as I have collected them piecemeal from John Campbell and his family and friends.

❧

IN THE LAST WEEKS OF AUGUST IN 1906 three men rode southwest across the Warm Springs Indian Reservation and into the Cascade Mountains south of Mt. Jefferson. No doubt they were leading a packhorse or two laden with their gear and food. They were an oddly assorted trio. The youngest was John Campbell, the eighteen-year-old red-haired oldest son of a pioneer rancher, Ed Campbell, who had homesteaded in the 1880s directly across the Deschutes River from the Reservation, and for years operated the only ferry on this stretch of the river. The second was a homesteader in his late thirties named Frank Stangland, whose wife had died suddenly of typhoid fever on the farm just the year before, in 1905, leaving him with three small children, who were promptly sent back to Indiana to live with their maternal grandparents. The third rider was a very tall Wasco Indian, about sixty, named Jim Polk.

The aim of the journey—what they told their families and friends and each other—was to hunt deer as they went and make jerky of the meat, and at the far end of the trip, southwest of the mountain known as the South Sister, to find and mine gold in a glacial stream called "Quartz Creek," where, according to a Wasco story told by Jim Polk, some of his people once found gold nuggets.

Along the way, probably for two weeks or more and into the month of September, Jim Polk held forth as expedition leader, indoctrinating his Anglo companions in the old Wasco ways of mountain travel and hunting. At night, camped along timbered lakes, he told them about the "Stick Indians," mischievous mountain spirits known to dwell in certain high gloomy places and capable of reading travelers' minds and luring them off the trail to their grief, unless placated by gifts of matches and bacon. At twilight, Jim Polk drew his friends' attention to what he identified as the soft, plaintive cries of the Stick Indians, and in the morning he pointed out, along the damp sand of the lakeshores, what he said were their small footprints.

Back on the trail and heading south each day, he showed his companions the traditional Indian system of trail markers, oddly broken and bent branches, twigs stuck in the ground, and so on, and interpreted them: "Three men and two women came this way … good berry patch above the next lake…" And most of all, Jim Polk took pains to show his comrades the intricate network of old-time Indian trails running obscurely, mostly without blazes, all over both sides of the mountains—into hidden coves and lakes, around impenetrable blow-downs, along narrow ridges above rock slides.

Occasionally they met other travelers, all Indians. None would speak English, but chattered in *kikscht* (Wasco) or Chinook Jargon, while glancing at Campbell and Stangland as they talked. Once, as the two white men prepared to illegally shoot an elk calf for a little fresh "camp meat," Jim Polk suddenly stopped them, saying that he knew that the government ranger at the little settlement at McKenzie Bridge thirty miles to the west would arrest them all if they proceeded. (Later, on their way home, when they detoured to McKenzie Bridge to buy provisions, the ranger praised them for resisting the temptation to kill that elk calf! "I'd of had to send you boys to the Pen for that!" How he knew, neither he nor Jim Polk would say.)

At length, leading their horses more often than riding, they followed a steep track running west above timberline, and came out on the high barren saddle between the Middle Sister and the South. Before them, seven or eight miles off to the west/southwest, a series of whitewater streams ran out of the tails of the glaciers and into very deep, steep-sided timbered canyons. One of these, "Quartz Creek," held gold nuggets, or so the story promised.

But that night, a light September snowstorm blew up out of the southwest, and although the snow had mostly melted before breakfast, Jim Polk announced to his friends that he would take them no further. Where they were heading, he said, there was a deep basin where, he now remembered, a bad thing once happened to some Wasco hunters. One of them shot a bear, and when it crawled into a cave, he pursued it and tried to drag it out, in violation of a hunting tabu. As a result, an early blizzard came up and trapped the party in the basin, and those who lived through that awful winter did so, it was said, by eating human flesh. *Bad medicine, hyas mesachie,* he said: "This little snow was sent to us as a warning, to stay away from that place and go home." So the three turned around, and after detouring west to McKenzie Bridge for supplies, and talking to the ranger there, they headed back east over the mountains and into central Oregon.

As they crossed the divide for the last time and started down into the timber, bound for home, Jim Polk turned in his saddle to look back at the rocks and snow they'd just come through, and murmured, "Good— the old ones didn't want us up there anyway!"

❖

NOW I HAVE ASSEMBLED THIS VERSION out of all the events and details of the story that I can recollect from John Campbell's partial tellings of it, and in doing so I have tried—perversely, unlike a crafty storyteller!—to maintain a neutral tone. Perhaps we can now say, "The real story might have been *something* like this," but still, if we liken the idea of narrative form to a bag, it's obvious that this bag can hardly stand upright, it's so underfilled with expressive content. So now we must turn to extra-narrative considerations, especially biography, local history, and anthropology, and attempt to eke out inferential connections between such extraneous detail and the story as we have it.

Who were these three men? Remarkably, one of them has been described at length in a recent book. In her memoir of central Oregon homesteading life, *Some Bright Morning,* Bess Stangland Raber rather bitterly characterizes her father Frank as insatiably curious, impulsive, cheerfully neglectful of his famly, utterly improvident as a homesteader.[5] Her harsh portrait is no doubt colored by the trauma of her mother's sudden illness and death in 1905, when Bess was a small girl, and by the subsequent "rescue" of her and her brothers by their mother's disapproving parents in Indiana, where they remained until adolescence, when they were allowed to return to Oregon. So Bess Stangland Raber's judgments of her father as he was around 1905 are probably suspect, but three or four images of him in her book *do* seem to amplify his role in our story.

(1) She reports that he was very friendly with John Campbell's family, and that in fact she and her brothers were taken in by the Campbells, after their mother's death and before they were sent back to their grandparents. (One might conjecture that in the eyes of John Campbell's parents, given their friendship with Frank Stangland, Frank was welcome on the 1906 adventure as a kind of chaperone for their son.) (2) Mrs.

---

5. Bess Stangland Raber, *Some Bright Morning* (Bend: Maverick Press, 1983), Chapters 30 and 34.

Raber characterizes her father as an avid naturalist, a great collector of "specimens" and a student of natural and Indian lore—which is precisely how I remember him in the 1940s as a kindly old retired farmer, very studious, still living on his tumbledown homestead with his second wife. (3) Mrs. Raber recalls that he was fascinated by stories of "lost" gold deposits, like the legendary Lost Blue Bucket Mine of eastern Oregon, and she offers a photo (p. 251) of him with a pack-string in snow, with the caption "Papa on a combination deer-hunting and gold-finding expedition into the Cascades in 1913." Was he headed back to Quartz Creek, seven years after his interrupted journey there with John Campbell and Jim Polk? (4) She indicates how her father was devastated by the death of his young wife Mabel in the spring of 1905, and remained distracted by grief and perhaps guilt for years afterward, alone on the homestead while his children were growing up in Indiana and being taught to disapprove of their father.

Now, does the saggy bag of our story stand up a little straighter? I think so. At least a conjectural picture of Frank Stangland and his motives in 1906 has emerged: of someone still burdened by the loss of both wife and children, lonesome, eager to leave his farm and light out for the mountains not only because he temperamentally preferred adventure to homesteading, but because the homestead was, only a year after his wife's death, a place of painful memories. And it's clear that, of the three travelers, Frank Stangland would have been the one most captivated by the prospect of gold somewhere over the Cascade Range.

About Jim Polk, I have found very little solid information outside of his role in the story as the expedition's guide, trail-boss, and spiritual leader. John Campbell always referred to him fondly and respectfully as "*old* Jim Polk." But according to Indian Service records, there were actually *two* Jim Polks, both alive in 1906. The elder was born in either 1845 or 1848, and is recorded as having enlisted as a military scout in the Paiute Wars of 1866 and again in the Modoc War of 1872. In Keith and Donna Clark's edition of Dr. William McKay's journal of the former campaign, he is listed as twenty-one years old, a resident of Warm Springs, by occupation a carpenter, and discharged as a private after service "in the Snake Wars." Later, he is listed as having served as an Army Scout in the Modoc War.[6] By both official account and hearsay, he was unusually tall—in fact a giant by Wasco standards, six feet two or even taller. The

---

6. Personal correspondence from David and Kathrine French, February 18, 1990, from their Warm Springs research files. The help of the Frenches has been indispensable to this essay.

fact that he is not listed in the 1915 Warm Springs census indicates that he had died before that year. His son James Polk Jr. is listed as having been born in 1869; he was living in the 1920s, but is not mentioned in a 1934 census, and can be assumed to have been dead by then. Which Jim Polk is our man?

All evidence in the story strongly points to the father. The son would have been only about thirty-seven at the time of John Campbell's adventure, no older in fact than Frank Stangland—hardly old enough to merit John's veneration of an "old" Jim Polk. Jim Sr. would, on the other hand, have been around sixty in 1906, "old" to an eighteen-year-old boy, but not necessarily decrepit, although it appears that he did die within a decade. His year of birth, whether 1845 or 1848, has a special significance. He would have been a small boy in 1855, the year his people, the Wascos, were forced by treaty to leave their Columbia River villages and join the Warm Springs Sahaptins on the newly created Warm Springs Reservation. According to some Wasco traditions, their hunting and gathering parties had been visiting this region and on south along the Cascades since time immemorial (which seasonal occupation became the U.S. government's rationale for "giving" them the land), but the elder Jim Polk's generation would have been the first to grow up on the reservation, and know its rugged terrain intimately as homeland. And of course it was his generation of young men coming of age in the 1860s and 1870s who earned historical recognition and a certain heroic status locally by helping the U.S. Army to quell their old tribal enemies the Paiutes, and, later, the Modocs.

So—picture an elderly man, strikingly tall, with a rather romantic past, involving a boyhood in the earliest years of the reservation, and military service against Indian "hostiles" in eastern Oregon and northern California. The appeal of such a figure for an eighteen-year-old farm boy is obvious; but what about Jim Polk's interest in young Johnny Campbell? It's known that Polk had several sons, his namesake and at least two others, all of them presumably products of Agency schooling and other Anglo acculturative influences, all of them grown by 1906. Did Jim Polk Sr. take on young John as a kind of surrogate son or nephew, someone eager and apt, albeit a white-eyes, to whom he could pass on the traditional lore and experience, hunting codes and so on, that Wasco men were supposed to pass on to their sons and nephews? The last time I heard John refer to "old Jim Polk," just before his death in 1978, he seemed to affirm some such special relationship: "Jim would always open up with me, but never with my dad or other white folks his own age."

As for John Campbell, when I knew him fifty years and more after his adventure, he was one of nature's aristocrats, a robust, genial, and exceptionally keen-minded old man who was revered by Anglos and Indians alike. His white neighbors recognized him as one of the builders of central Oregon; he'd had a constructive hand, it seems, in every public advance in the Madras area, and he carried the region's unwritten history infallibly in his head—a personal history now mostly lost, I must add, except *ex post facto* for notations like this one. Amongst the older Indians, his name was like magic; I doubt that any white man was ever more universally liked and trusted by the traditional people at Warm Springs. Their byword was: "If Johnny Campbell says it's so, it's *hyas kloshe, OK!*" They saw him as one of their own, and I'd like to think that his special identity with the Indians began to take shape in the summer of 1906 under the tutelage of Jim Polk Sr., in the tall timber and foothills of the Cascade Mountains.

Like nearly all American Indian groups, the traditional Wascos followed the custom of the spirit quest, wherein adolescents of both sexes were sent out alone into the mountains to fast and meditate, until they had a visionary encounter with the supernatural animal or natural force that would be their secret guardian and identity-sponsor for the rest of their lives. Probably John Campbell, who was not a romantic, would blush at the suggestion, but I'll offer it anyway: that his journey with Frank Stangland and Jim Polk amounted to a kind of protracted cross-cultural spirit quest and initiation rite, guided on the one hand, perhaps, by an at-loose-ends Anglo widower, and on the other hand, by an Indian elder who knew where all the trails went.

Certainly a pattern was established: for the rest of his active life, when work and domestic demands permitted, John delighted in making late-summer packtrips into the central Oregon Cascades, at first over the fading Native trails, and later over the U.S. Forest Service trail systems (built by the Civilian Conservation Corps in the 1930s). On that first trip, back in 1906, the real gold for John Campbell must have been what he found, and was shown, along the way.

Now our attempt to contextualize his story must turn directly to geographical and anthropological considerations. John Campbell never pinpointed the location of "Quartz Creek" on a map, and its location is unknown to me; but a few years after his death I happened to notice on the standard U.S. Forest Service map of the Three Sisters Wilderness Area, southwest of the South Sister, near the glacial head of Separation Creek, and just about where, apparently, he and his comrades expected to find gold, an odd notation: "Indian Holes." No one in the local Forest Service offices could tell me what the term meant, or where it came from, so in July 1989 my brother Jim and I hiked in to see for ourselves. The country is very rough, and about as remote from roads as any place in Oregon, but it is spectacularly beautiful in late July, with very deep ravines running down from the western flanks of the South Sister, each with its own glacial torrent running through lush meadows waist high in grass and alpine wildflowers—Indian paintbrush, Cascade lilies, shooting stars, spirea, squaw grass—and springs pouring out of every hillside. All of one's glances to the east and north are challenged by the bulk of the South Sister, so much gray rock and glistening ice filling the eye.

Not knowing what "Indian Holes" specified, we aimlessly clambered around all afternoon, up ridges and down into meadows again, wondering if "holes" meant sinkholes or maybe volcanic "blowouts," or maybe even something the Indians had carved or dug—but we found nothing of the sort. Finally it dawned on us that these small alpine meadows, mostly circular and ringed by tall evergreens, looked from the ridges above very much like holes: holes in the landscape. And confirming the "Indian" part of their identity on the map, we found two telltale signs: an amazing concentration of deer and elk, so heavy that the stench of their fresh manure was overpowering; and, glinting in the sun alongside an elk-turd on the freshly turned earth of a gopher mound, a well-flaked obsidian hide-scraper.

With this artifact in view (but sad to tell, no gold nuggets), the puzzle of "Indian Holes" and its connection with John Campbell's story began to unravel. Clearly, judging from what we found in 1989, the region would have been a paradise for hunting deer and elk. And, on the other hand, looking upslope from the meadows at the bottom of any of the "holes," it was easy to imagine how a sudden heavy snowstorm would make escape virtually impossible. The story about the trapped hunters that spooked Jim Polk now looked entirely plausible.[7]

As my brother and I consulted our map in preparation to return to the trailhead on Foley Ridge to the northwest, we noted that only a few miles northeast of Indian Holes are the Obsidian Cliffs, well-known as an ancient Indian source of high-quality volcanic glass for making

---

7. One of John Campbell's sisters, the late Mrs. Lou Murray of Medford, Oregon, recalled a somewhat different version of this episode. In her account, the three men actually camped at Indian Holes, and Jim Polk inexplicably disappeared from camp for a day and a night, returning, apparently, just before the snowstorm that sent him and his companions on their way

weapons and tools. And about midway betwen Obsidian Cliffs and Indian Holes, our map specified another intriguing feature: "Racetrack Meadows." There wasn't time on this hike to check it out—as my brother remarked, not impatiently, no wild-goose chase should try to find all of its geese at once—but I resolved to come back sooner or later, to see if, as I suspected, "Racetrack Meadows" in fact marks the site of an old-time Indian racetrack and summer campground, of which several are known in the Oregon and Washington Cascades, invariably in high alpine settings, rich in game, as here.

The most celebrated of these grounds is located at the southern edge of the so-called "Indian Heaven" country, south of Mt. Adams, in Washington State. Across a hidden basin, full of jewel-like meadows and streams, a well-marked track runs, surveyor-straight, for about a quarter of a mile, the dirt on it so compacted by horse hooves that no vegetation grows on it to this day. At each end, the track loops off the flat and up on the hillside for a few yards, presumably allowing the Indian jockeys to make a grand turnaround and then gallop back down the track the other way.

According to documented Indian traditions, the race-grounds at "Indian Heaven" were in use long before the whites came, serving as a gathering point late each summer for tribes from east and west of the mountains. To stand at one end of the racetrack and survey the scene even now is to know instinctively what such occupations must have been like: the racket of dogs and children; lodges and campfires scattered over the basin; preparation of deer and elk meat and huckleberries for the long winter to come; rings of gamblers chanting as the bones passed from hand to hand; much intertribal flirtation and hanky-panky; and everywhere, the celebration of good horseflesh—showing it off, trading it, and of course racing it for high stakes and family honor.[8]

It must have been life at the brim by Native standards, carefree and joyously sociable. Such happy conjectures were much in my mind, then, in late July 1990, as I hiked in from Foley Ridge to inspect Racetrack Meadow. What I found there, at the intersection of several USFS trails, vividly confirmed the supposition of extensive and long-standing Indian summer occupation: concentrated scatterings of obsidian flakes and shards, along with a few unfinished arrowpoints and hide-scrapers, clearly marked off camping sites in sandy areas around the meadow. The meadow itself, about forty acres in size, is apparently an old meltwater lakebed,

---

8. See Mel Hansen, *Indian Heaven Back Country* (Portland: Touchstone Press, 1977).

very flat and covered with gravel and sparse vegetation—perfect for running horses, whereas most alpine meadows (like those at Indian Holes) are broken up with streambeds, animal burrows, and dense, clumpy vegetation, and thus unsatisfactory (in fact downright unsafe) for serious racing. I found no "racetrack" per se, equivalent to the indelible scar at the Indian Heaven site in Washington State; but it appears very likely that the USFS trail running north/south across the meadow (No. 3547B) simply follows the old track.

Overall, the impression of very old, very intensive occupation is strong here, and it is good to note that the Forest Service has lately begun to study its archaeological significance. At Warm Springs, there is very little recollection of summer occupations in this area, suggesting that they must have stopped several generations ago, before the turn of the century—perhaps in part because the huckleberry patches had begun to recede (berries are hard to find there now), and of course because, with the advent of firearms and other metal implements, the need for obsidian for weapons and tools ended abruptly, soon after the Civil War.[9]

In any event, what we seem to have found is an unexpected piece of Indian ethnohistory embedded in a white pioneer's story, and perhaps in turn illuminating it. One wonders who was more disappointed at not reaching Indian Holes and "Quartz Creek"—Frank Stangland, with his hopes of finding gold, or Jim Polk, with what must have been a powerful urge to return one more time, even in mixed company, to his people's old summer playground. Somehow I can't believe that young John Campbell was much disappointed in anything, going or coming.

At this point, further pursuit of the circumstances of what became his story, such as it is, would have to take a purely speculative, fictive slant. What did they eat, those three? Did they really take the time and trouble to prepare jerky? What did they talk about around the fire? Was Frank Stangland more and more the "odd man out" of the trio, with the old Indian and the Anglo boy increasingly paired off as mentor and protégé? Was Jim Polk's authority in calling off the final trek to the supposed gold site challenged by either of his companions? And when they finally got back to the Warm Springs Agency and separated, how did they say goodbye to each other? Given how, as Robert Frost says,

9. One of David and Kathrine French's Warm Springs acquaintances recalled going up into the Three Sisters country in the 1930s, to an area known at Warm Springs as "The Sugar Bowl," to pick huckleberries, but she added that the berry patches were scattered, and too far from camp. (Personal correspondence, February 18, 1990)

"way leads on to way," did the three of them ever meet again, to reminisce about their adventure?

Such speculations are, of course, the irresistible imaginative consequence of all stories, from "The Three Little Pigs" to *War and Peace*, a kind of interpretive residue, and if unaccountable, they are not to be dismissed out of hand, for they do indicate something about the mysterious way a story takes dominion in our minds, one explicit detail evoking or seeming to preclude the possibility of others. "How many children had Lady Macbeth?" "Where did Lear's Fool go?" These used to be questions that the "New Critics" taunted their scholarly elders with, as examples of fruitless and unwarranted extratextual conjecture, but in many years of teaching Shakespeare I've never taught a class in which these and similar questions haven't been honestly raised, and now I think they should be heeded, at least on a narratological basis. Shakespeare doesn't tell us the answers about Lady Macbeth's mysterious infants, might even regret that he didn't take better care to preclude our being distracted (mostly in reading) by such queries, but the fact that we do indulge in such extratextual speculation is a healthy and, I would say, honorable confirmation that we are actually engaging a story, sorting it out as it occupies our minds.

Given the very scanty assortment of narrative detail in John Campbell's tale, however, even after contextualization, it would be easy to overwhelm it with speculation; anyway, that way lies the kind of fictive reinvention that I proposed to avoid at the outset. If we must speculate, better to do so about how, according to what storytelling strategies and conventions, the tale might begin in some "full-dress" performance, of the sort it has never received. For example, should we begin:

"It was a dark and stormy night, snowing in fact, and Jim Polk told his friends, 'Boys, we won't go no further. …' "

Or: "On August 18, 1906, at about three in the afternoon, a casual observer might have discerned three riders and two packhorses setting off up Shitike Creek in the shimmering heat, for the mountains. Their destination: gold."

Or: "Sing in me, Muse, and through me tell the story nearly forgotten, of those three heroic riders, who wandered …"

Or: "Coyote was going there, and he saw this poor mutilated story limping down the trail, with some people following it, and he said to himself, 'Aha!' "

In any event, in conclusion I want to briefly turn back to what the tale gives us to know about its elements, my purpose now being directly *interpretive*—what do these elements add up to in their given order? We've already noted the historical and archetypal patterns of meaning, the first having to do with Indian/white relationships at the turn of the century, and the second bearing on John Campbell's coming into manhood. That personal focus—it is, after all, now and forever *his* story, not that of his companions—expresses itself in the tonality or "atmosphere" of the narrative. If it's possible to talk about tone without recourse to a fixed verbal text (and I think it is), I'd characterize that tone as spooky, uncanny, *unheimlich*. The terrain is by implication increasingly remote and unfamiliar to John Campbell and Frank Stangland, at least, and their guide through it is an elder not of their own race and culture, who adduces the presence of "Stick Indians," mischievous nocturnal spirits affiliated by name and belief with the Wasco Indians, but "other" even to them, and local to the country at hand. The increasing strangeness of it all climaxes, of course, in Polk's unexpected reaction to the brief snowstorm, just before they reach their avowed destination. His decision to turn back because of a recollection of the hunters' grisly predicament in the basin years before, resulting from their violation of some hunting taboo, must have seemed unaccountable, otherwordly to his Anglo companions. And even after this unsettling reversal, the narrative's spooky tonality persists, as in the discovery, when they visit McKenzie Bridge on the way home, that the Ranger somehow knew that Frank and John had intended to kill an elk-calf out of season.

This last detail, suggesting telepathy, is one of several evoking a special kind of uncanniness by emphasizing alien forms of language. Presumably Jim Polk spoke a form of English to his companions, but on the trail they meet Indian travelers, who converse with Polk only in Native languages, obviously commenting on the two whites, but unintelligibly. Even more unnerving, perhaps, is the observation that the Stick Indians understand human thoughts without speech, and treacherously try to "communicate" with people in the language of birds. And Jim Polk's disclosure of a Native "language" of trail signs opens up a whole new area of foreign, nonverbal discourse, potentially crucial to the safety and well-being of the expedition, but at first, at least, only Jim Polk knows how to read the signs.[10] This pattern and its unsettling effect continues

---

10. This is one of only two references to Northwest Native trail signs known to me. The other appears in Henry L. Abbot's account of his travels through central Oregon in 1854-55 in search

right to the final scene, in which Polk, relieved to be out of the mountains and perhaps still a little spooked by the ominous snowstorm near Indian Holes, appears to render in English a private communication he's had with the spirits of the region, to the effect that the travelers were unwelcome all along: "Good—the old ones didn't want us up there anyway!"

The pattern is striking in a narrative with so few expressive details, and its effect serves, I think, to draw attention to John Campbell's equivocal situation as a sort of initiate into the mysteries of adult life, or more precisely as a young white spirit-quester in an Indian context. The weird and uncanny qualities of his experience seem to correspond to what the anthropologist Victor Turner calls the experience of "liminality" in initiation rituals and rites of passage around the world. Liminality means "at the threshhold"; according to Turner, initiation rituals "put the initiand temporarily into close rapport with the primary or primordial powers of the cosmos, the acts of which transcend rather than transgress the norms of human secular society." Liminality is "pure potency, where anything can happen, where immoderacy is normal, even normative, and where the elements of culture and society are released from their customary configurations and recombine in bizarre and terrifying imagery."[11]

If Turner's language here is a little too sweeping and melodramatic for John Campbell's narrative, at least as we have it, the concept of liminality as a phase of initiatory experience does seem to apply, usefully. The weirdness of this initiation episode, of course, is colored by the fact that it is a transcultural experience, more Indian, in fact, than Anglo. Even though the ostensible goal of the trip is the thoroughly Anglo one of "finding gold," both the goal and the way to it are defined in Indian terms, and—pushing the plot to its symbolic limits, perhaps—the failure of John Campbell to actually reach such a goal may indicate that it was not a real or worthy goal for him, anyway. The pattern here is a familiar one in tales of youthful adventures and quests in world folklore: the Quester comes home with empty pockets but wonderfully, permanently

---

of possible railroad routes. In following Indian trails, he noted that "we had occasionally seen blazing, and sometimes twigs broken in the direction of the trail. The blazing generally consisted of a single cut, laying bare the wood; but sometimes we found a rude image of a man marked in the bark. This always indicated that much fallen timber was to be expected ..." (*Reports of Explorations and Surveys to Ascertain the Most Practical and Economical Route for a Railroad from the Mississippi River to the Pacific Ocean*, Vol. VI (Washington D.C.: War Department, 1857), p. 99.

11. Victor Turner, "Myth and Symbol," in *International Encyclopedia of Social Sciences*, Vol.8 (New York: Macmillan, 1968), p. 577 ff.

enriched by his experiences along the way. John Campbell doesn't find gold nuggets, nor does he seem to attain an adult Indian identity or spirit guardian, but he does acquire, maybe, a lifelong Native perspective, especially on how one belongs to one's homeland. A more fully developed narrative would, I conjecture, play off what John learns against what Frank Stangland is too old and set in Anglo experience (and perhaps too distracted by grief) to learn, and against what Jim Polk *knows* as a Wasco elder, someone who foresees the imminent loss of such knowledge amongst those who live in his homeland, both Indians and Anglos.

Our story presents one other structural pattern, notice of which will bring our "meta-narrative" enterprise full circle and to a close. Having labored to compose a kind of secondary story around John Campbell's primary tale, in order to bring out and consolidate its features, I want to point out something that you may have already recognized: that, as embryonic as it is, the primary plot contains and in fact crucially turns on two interior stories, both of them from Indian oral tradition. Campbell's tale begins, remember, with mention of the tale about the Wascos' discovery of gold in the mountains, which provides our travelers with their official purpose to travel; and it reaches its climax and point of reversal with Jim Polk's reference to the disaster of the snowbound hunters, which, used by Polk as a cautionary tale, frustrates the travelers' purpose and sends them home.

It seems strange, though ultimately appropriate, to find that a rudimentary story whose very integrity we have been trying to identify and conserve, contains within itself, egg-like, two interior narratives. But this configuration, one of whose effects is always to make us self-conscious that we are in the domain of Story, is of course no more than typical of the magic and power of storytelling. Perhaps we have stories within stories within stories, one level interacting with another, because we need narrative emblems to show that reality is often concentric in meaning, target-like: worlds within worlds within worlds, John Campbell's boyhood experience within the full completed circle of his long life, and that within the unfinished orbits of your life and mine, and so on. All of which maybe suggests why we have stories in the first place, as moving emblems of life conjoining the local and the universal, the "what is" and the "what might be"; and why conserving stories of all sorts is a necessary kind of ecology; and why I've wanted you to have John Campbell's story in the first place, so far as it was ever mine to give.

Three

GOING AROUND THE MOUNTAIN

I

THROUGH MUCH OF CENTRAL OREGON, from the Mutton Mountains south into Deschutes County, Mt. Jefferson is the commanding landmark to the west, the magnetic pole of our mental compasses. Wherever I've traveled, I've always located "west" by closing my eyes and visualizing Jefferson's sharp-edged peak, and then imposing it on whatever landscape or cityscape I'm in. Doing this doesn't always get me oriented, admittedly—but it's still a reassuring ritual in foreign spaces.

It's a mystery how such a landmark can be so immediate and familiar, part of the furniture of one's everyday life, and yet seem at times utterly remote and strange. In the case of Mt. Jefferson, this may be in part a trick of light. From our home-place on Agency Plains, the mountain stands a good thirty miles away by crow's flight, and in the full midday glare of summer it generally looks like it's at least that far away, although still the highest eminence on the western horizon. But on a dark day, or at dusk, especially with some clouds behind it, it can loom up blue-black and alarmingly close, a different mountain altogether. No doubt this illusion, working on a newcomer's ignorance of the scale of our Western landscapes, was what inspired a Ramsey cousin visiting from Missouri to announce one overcast morning that he was going to hike over to that mountain, there, and would try to be back in time for dinner. Whichever relative was telling this story always added, scornfully, "They should of let him try it!"

Like a latterday druid keeping track of the sun's seasonal course, my father religiously marked where it disappeared at sunset behind Jefferson's flanks, and told us when, after the summer solstice, it began to backtrack southward in its settings. Just the other day I found a note he'd scribbled to himself, on September 28, 1972: "Sun passed to set on south side of Mt. Jeff." On such seasonal passages, he would invariably announce, "Days will be shorter from now on," maybe to persuade us to put out more honest work in the ever-decreasing daylight hours ahead. When he and my mother undertook some improvements on our old house in the 1950s, one of the highlights was a big "picture window" that spectacularly framed Mt. Jefferson in the dining room's west wall.

Given its prominence in our everyday lives, then, it's not surprising that at vacation time in August, after wheat harvest, we (and other families) often went camping "up in the mountains," usually in Jefferson's southern foothills above the Metolius River, especially at a lovely Forest Service camp on Abbot Creek. But for a stretch in the 1940s, our pilgrimatic approaches to the mountain took a much more strenuous course, at least for Dad and Jim, who mounted horseback "pack-trips" into the Mt. Jefferson Wilderness; and in 1949 the four of us joined Lloyd and Thelma Luelling and their two boys in an epical two-week circumnavigation of the whole mountain. In retelling that story, I am indebted to a short but vivid log my mother kept of the trip, augmented by notes written by Lloyd Luelling in 1977, shortly before his death.

I don't know when exactly my dad and his childhood friend Lloyd began to hatch this ultimate expedition, but in effect they had been rehearsing it since 1941, when Dad and Jim made their first brief pack-trip with John Campbell into Jefferson's southern approaches. By then, Dad was already well into his new cattle-rancher mode. Besides the challenge of taking horses into the mountains and learning the technology of pack-saddles and *alforjas* or saddle-bags (we called them "alforkeses"), there was the challenge of mastering the trails around Mt. Jefferson. In those pre-backpacking days they consisted of (1) the well-maintained official "Skyline Trail" (now the Pacific Crest Trail), which ran as high as possible around Jefferson's north, west, and south sides; (2) various blazed Forest Service and CCC trails dating back to the twenties and thirties, mostly unmaintained; (3) old Indian trails, unblazed, unmaintained, and likely to appear suddenly in dense timber and peter out in a thicket. From a lifetime of exploring this country, often with Indians from the Warm Springs Reservation, John Campbell was the acknowledged expert on trails in the mountains.

In 1942, he, Dad, and Jim went back to the mountain with Dad's older brother Leslie and his son Leslie Jr.; and in 1944 and 1945 (as if asserting full pack-trip mastery) Dad and Jim went without John Campbell, but added two real tenderfeet, our neighbor Floyd Evick and an irrepressible Madras grocer, Jeff Murray, who managed to kill a very old black bear out of season and brought its mangy hide back home as a trophy.

Maybe it was the rough edges and macho tensions of these last two trips that suggested the idea of a *family* expedition, in company with the Luellings. If so, there was a memorable Ramsey-family precedent for such an undertaking. In the summer of 1910, less than a decade after Grandpa and Grandma had claimed their homestead in central Oregon, two of Grandpa's grown children and their families came out from Missouri to see the new frontier, and nothing would do but for Grandpa to mount a summer-long odyssey by buggy and trap-wagon over the mountains, across the Willamette Valley, through the Coast Range, to show the Missourians the Oregon Coast. The older children, some nearly grown, were left at home to attend to harvest, while Grandpa and Grandma and their two youngest, my father (five) and his baby sister, Bea, went off with the visitors. Their adventure lasted nearly all summer, like a late reenactment of the Oregon Trail within the boundaries of Oregon; my dad used to recall their paying a toll to use the west segment of the famous emigrant "Barlow Road" over the west flank of Mt. Hood. I've always suspected that memories of *his* father intrepidly leading the way as family wagonmaster in 1910 colored Dad's planning of our 1949 trip. He was established then and thereafter as our wagonmaster—except that we didn't have any wagons.

As the plan unfolded for us in the spring and summer of that year, it took the form of a one hundred-mile loop completely around Mt. Jefferson, beginning at "Peter's Pasture," an old CCC camp on Shitike Creek on the Warm Springs Reservation, climbing southwest into Kuckup Park and then picturesque Jefferson Park directly under the mountain's north face; thence on the Skyline Trail around the west side to Pamelia Lake; up the zig-zag summit trail of Grizzly Peak and then down off-trail to Grizzly Flats. From here we would go cross-country east and south on old Indian trails (if we could find them) over Jefferson's south flank to a plateau known as the Table; then connect with Forest Service trails leading south and east below the Cascade crest to Carl and Cabot lakes, and finally out to civilization, in the form of our favorite campground at Abbot Creek. The actual loop would be completed only by Dad, Jim, and Lloyd, who would ride (with the pack-animals) all the way from home to Peter's Pasture, meeting the rest of us there; and then, at the far end, once we all reached Abbot Creek (where trucks would be waiting), they would finish the loop by riding around the bend of the Metolius River and across the Warm Springs Reservation by way of Seekseekwa, Tenino, and Shitike creeks, and so on home. Some outing!

Who were we? As we packed up and prepared to leave Peter's Pasture the morning of August 19, 1949, we were eight humans, eight saddle horses, two dogs, four mules, and a burro. More exactly:

A. S. "Gus" Ramsey, forty-four, riding Traveller
Wilma Ramsey, forty-three, on Flicka
Jim Ramsey, seventeen, on ???? (a borrowed horse)
Jerry Ramsey, eleven, on Dolly
"Duffy," Ramsey family dog, middle-aged

Lloyd Luelling, forty-five, riding Snip
Thelma Luelling, forty-three, on Topsy
Lee Luelling, nine, on Sandy
Tommy Luelling, six, on Fox
"Freckles," Luelling family dog, adolescent

The pack-string of mules (borrowed from various
     Indian friends):
Dave
John
Jack
Queenie
plus a burro, pressed upon us by a friend: Geranium

Our two families went way back in friendship, although they were Missionary Baptists, and we were Methodists. Dad and Lloyd had been helping each other with their cattle, at branding time and on the Marginal Land pastures, for years. Lloyd was very religious but easygoing, and irresistably enthusiastic; my dad tended to be stern and a perfectionist—theirs was a working friendship of complementary opposites. Thelma and my mother were well-matched for the adventure in being even-tempered and cheerful, and also in *not* being seasoned equestriennes.

The Luelling boys Lee and Tommy (baby brother Mark would be left with relatives) were not schoolmates of mine, but we sometimes played together at the joint family roundups. Lee was dark-haired and very serious; Tommy was blond and a lovable roughneck comedian, willing to try anything with or without a dare. Neither shared my current obsession with model airplanes and reading, but we had enough in common to be pals. There was no one on the Luelling side to tally with my older brother Jim, but at seventeen he was already his own man, and as an experienced horseman and trail-rider he had the satisfaction of being included, most of the time, in the ranks of the "menfolks."

Rounding out the entourage and campfire circle were our two dogs—good friends, too, happily, except that their Freckles was much younger than our black dog Duffy, who tried his best to keep up with Freckles on every chipmunk chase around the mountain, and was never quite the same dog after the trip was over.

By D-Day (as we called it) we were equipped with sleeping bags and bedrolls and heavy canvas tarps, but no tents. On the mules' pack-saddles and alforkeses we would be carrying staple provisions enough for two weeks—bags of biscuit and pancake flour, fifteen dozen eggs, oatmeal, ham and bacon, coffee, canned milk, canned vegetables, fruit, and meat, potatoes, fresh ears of corn, and carrots. Geranium, the burro, would tote the pots and pans. We had between us two cameras, no radios, possibly a compass, a war-surplus medicine kit, fishing tackle, a shovel and an axe or two, and one firearm, my dad's .22-caliber automatic pistol. This cargo would have to be enough; Dad and Lloyd said it would do. So we were ready at last!

II

The question whether to take pack-horses on a camping trip is one that cannot be completely settled, one way or the other. They can keep going in country where the best four-wheel drive truck would be helpless, but they have to be grazed, watered, and watched against straying, fighting, stampeding, and running away, so that half the time it is open to debate whether they are not more trouble than they are worth. It depends on what one gets out of the trip, probably. If it turns out to have been worth taking, the horses are not enough to spoil it. Emergencies are bound to come up, and getting the best of all of them would be like watching a horse race with the results posted at the start, or fighting a war with bean bags tied to sticks. One has to risk losing for winning to mean anything.

I am inclined to think, looking back over a good many years spent at it, that though a large part of the good one derives from camping is in triumphing over its incidental emergencies, an even larger part is the emergencies themselves, win or lose.

H.L. Davis, "The Camp," in *Kettle of Fire*

"THOSE GODDAM MULES AGAIN!"

H .L. Davis is philosophizing here about packing with *horses*, and it's an open question whether he would have been so equanimous about packing *mules*—especially if he'd come along with us in 1949. That first morning's pack-up at Peter's Pasture took much longer than expected, and set the pattern for the rest of the trip. Dave, John, Jack, and Queenie—great tall lanky dark-bay creatures with outlandish ears and wicked eyes—kicked, bucked, bit, and otherwise resisted every effort to put the saddle blankets on their backs, and then the cross-framed wooden pack-saddles, and finally the heavy wooden and leather alforkeses themselves, laden with all our provisions and gear. What had been at dawn a peaceful, dew-wet forest campground was transformed into a dusty, noisy circus arena, as Dad, Lloyd, and Jim tried to get the job done.

The rest of us watched with uneasy interest from a safe distance; I was wondering how long it would be before my father's self-imposed ban on swearing would be violated. I didn't have long to wait. Finally, it was determined that "Dave" was the real source of the trouble, and he was led apart and snubbed up tight between two trees, to be saddled and packed separately. This drastic tactic worked (and it worked, more or less, throughout the trip, as long as we had two trees a Dave's-length apart). With the packs on all the mules, the tarps were thrown over them, the ropes were laced tightly over everything in the elegant packers' "diamond hitch," and we were ready for our adventure after all. We splashed gaily across Shitike Creek and set off, single file, up the trail to Kuckup Park.

No more than a quarter-mile up the trail, Queenie's pack began to loosen and slip; she pulled back and began to buck, and soon there was a tangle of jostling mules and lead-ropes in the middle of our caravan. Dad and Lloyd galloped back to intervene, but Queenie broke loose and headed into the timber, her pack now hanging under her belly. With every jump, the five-gallon tin cans in the alforkeses banged and crashed, making an ungodly racket, and spooking not only poor Queenie but the other mules and our horses, too. Dad and Lloyd galloped after Queenie, and the rest of us could hear the tin-pan-alley noise of their chase receding in the distance.

Meanwhile, we were busy at local damage control. Part of Queenie's cargo was the five-gallon can containing our entire egg supply, ingeniously packed in oats (for the horses). There was now a shocking trail of oats and eggs, many of them broken, marking Queenie's tormented flight into the woods. We hunkered down and sifted through the wreckage:

amazingly, we salvaged and repacked six or seven dozen eggs, and by that time the men had returned with poor Queenie and her pack-gear. A review of saddling and packing procedures ensued, and a check of the tightness of all saddles (it was discovered that Dave's was loose, too); and we were off again, ready for the next challenge.

I don't recall any further mishaps with loose pack-saddles—just that packing the mules became, every blessed time, a tense and violent operation, pitting resolute men against defiant beasts. I have to believe that Dad and Lloyd actually enjoyed these skirmishes; after all, they had invited Queenie, Dave, and Co. to come along in the first place. But Mom and I kept our distance from it all, and worried over what would happen next.

What happened next—repeatedly—was the realization of another possibility on H. L. Davis's list of reasons not to go camping with pack-animals: they tend to get loose and run away. Understand that on such an expedition into the wilds you can't just feed and water your animals each night and then tie them up: they have to be able to graze with some degree of freedom, and the grass in Mt. Jefferson's meadows was very tall and lush that year. So hobbles were used, and also long tether ropes tied to something. Neither form of restraint worked very well. And sometimes it was thought permissible to let the animals graze freely, under supervision, of course.

I surmised that our trailmasters' theoretical grasp of this critical point was seriously in advance of practical reality early on, when Lloyd enthusiastically showed his boys and me an old cowboy trick for picketing horses on the open range. We were standing with him and one of the horses, in the middle of a meadow. I noticed he was holding the camp-shovel. "Now boys, here's this hungry horse, but you can't just turn him loose to eat; how would you keep him from running off?" "Hit him with that shovel, Dad!" Tommy said. "No, son, but if you dig a hole with it, you'll solve the problem." So we took turns digging a deep hole, and Lloyd tied a bulky knot in the end of the tether-rope, dropped it into the hole, and tromped the sod back in on top of it. "Now try to pull it out-sideways, the way a horse would pull." We tugged and tugged, but couldn't budge it, and went off to play, impressed by this lesson in cowboy lore. When we checked on the horse a little later, however, the hole was empty, and the horse was unconcernedly dragging its tether at the far end of the meadow. ...

At any rate, and for whatever reason, the horses very nearly got away our very first night on the trail. A few nights later, at Grizzly Flats, the four mules made their first break-out, apparently aiming to go home to the Reservation. They very nearly made it, too. In our leisurely early-morning routine in an established camp like this one, we hadn't even missed them when they suddenly appeared, in company with John Campbell's son, John, and his wife, Gay, who were out on a little mountain excursion of their own. They'd met the mules several miles down the trail, "heads down and heading for home"—but apparently one of the mules recognized an Indian horse John was riding, and so they all turned around and followed our welcome visitors back to camp! How far can we go on such blind luck, I wondered.

No doubt hobbles and tethers were triple-checked, but the night that we arrived at our next camp, at Table Lake, Dave, John, Jack, and Queenie were rashly given a little freedom after their hard day's work, and promptly ran away again. An anxious night ensued. In her log, my mother wrote, "We all ate a hearty supper, then the men discovered that all of the mules were gone. They hunted for them until dark—but no luck. One mule has a bell on him—but no sound. We sort of scolded the men for turning the mules loose. We have had so many narrow escapes with them." Amazingly, we were granted yet another escape: we were awakened at dawn the next day by the clanging of the mule-bell, announcing the return of all of the mules, except for Dave.

I want to leave stubborn Dave out there in the woods for a bit, in order to pay my respects to the fifth member of our pack-string, Geranium the burro. Geranium had the irresistible fuzziness and also the inscrutable demeanor of a giant panda; Lee, Tommy, and I loved her, wreathed her head and neck with garlands of wild-flowers, surreptitiously fed her candy-bars and corn-cobs, and sympathized with her when she was bad and balky on the trail, reluctantly carrying her little pack of pots and pans. At least *she* didn't try to run away; Dad and Lloyd joked, maybe a little defensively, about how, if the mules left us for good, Geranium would get us home.

Who knows how she saw us through her big mournful eyes, as she moped every night on the edge of camp? Her one moment of self-expression, other than balking, came as we were leaving Jefferson Park. The day before, she had met another burro, named "Pancho," who had promptly kicked her in the rump. It must have been an act of burro flirtation, because when we left the Park and Geranium realized she was leaving Pancho's vicinity, she frantically tried to break loose and run back to him, and then hee-hawed heartbrokenly far on down the trail.

By the time we were on the last leg of the tour, her balkiness had become a serious problem, and even we boys were angry with her for holding up the parade so often. Finally, our last day out, on the long grade down from Carl Lake, she simply refused to go, her little hooves dug into the pine duff like shovels. So the men decided to leave her loosely tied up with some grain and water and take the rest of the caravan on out to Abbot Creek, and then come back for her. But when Dad returned, he was shocked to find her dead, right where we'd left her. She must have been sick with some internal malady, but, given her habitual unresponsiveness, how would we have known? If she had died early on, everybody would have been devastated, especially Tom, Lee, and me; but in the excitement of reaching the end of the trail, we shed a few tears for her, as boys will, and went on with our eager preparations to go home. I hope she forgives us our disloyalty.

Now I must retrieve David Mule, still strayed out there in the dense woods below our Table Lake camp. Doing so brings me to the episode known in our family as "the great bear barbecue." When the other mules returned that morning without Dave, Dad and Lloyd rode off to search for him in the really wild country below us to the east. They soon decided to separate to cover more ground. Hearing a suspicious noise in a thicket, and noticing that Traveller was nervously blowing and snorting, Dad dismounted and led him into the trees to look. All of a sudden he found himself face to face with a very large black bear, standing on her hind legs and showing her teeth. With an angry bear about to charge in front of him, and a spooked horse behind him, blocking his retreat, he pulled out his pistol and fired into the bear's maw. She crumpled at his feet. As he turned around to calm Traveller, he heard a noise above him, and saw two small cubs up a tree. Knowing that their mother's death had condemned them to a lingering death by starvation, he reluctantly shot them, too, and then extricated himself and his horse from the thicket and sat down to smoke and reflect on what he'd had to do.

Pretty soon, drawn by the gunfire, Lloyd rode up leading the lost mule, Dave. Seeing my dad's distress over having to kill the bears, he made a cheering proposal: "Gus, we'll have us an old-time Indian bear barbecue! We've been needing some fresh camp-meat, anyway!" So they bundled up the two cubs and tied them on the backs of their saddles, and rode back to camp.

I don't recall that my mother and Thelma responded with much enthusiasm, either to the sight of the cubs or the plan to barbecue them—especially not after they'd been skinned and dressed and laid out in a snowbank to cool off. But Lee, Tommy, and I were soon caught up in Lloyd's enthusiasm for the project. At his direction, we dug a deep pit near camp and then gathered wood and helped him build a fire in the pit. When the fire had burnt down to coals, the cuts of milk-white bear meat were wrapped up in fir-boughs and ferns, and placed on the coals, then wet gunny sacks were laid on, and then more boughs, and finally a layer of dirt to seal in the heat. Lloyd cheered us on: "Oh, it'll be a grand feast, just like the old people would have fixed up here. Four or five hours, and we'll have a real *hyas ipswoot muckamuck!*"

By late afternoon, we were famished, and the mounded-up pit had stopped steaming. Plates and silverware were readied, but when the fire-pit was uncovered, instead of the savory smell of roasted meat we expected, a sickly-sweet odor of scorched and steamed fir-boughs wafted up. Jim and I looked at one another … but Lloyd was already gleefully unwrapping the steaming cuts and carving them up for us. "Mmmm, doesn't get any better!" he pronounced after his first forkful—but in truth all I could taste was that rank sweetish fir-bough flavor: apparently the meat itself, rather like veal, had very little flavor of its own. It was dreadful, both the taste and the situation; I noticed my parents looking at their plates. When I covertly offered Duffy a piece, he sniffed at it and walked away. Meanwhile, polite noises were being made for the chef's benefit; clearly, it was one of those situations where the meal had to be served, and not the truth. Mercifully, the first whiffs of the opened barbecue pit had taken my appetite away, anyway, but I thought I could detect that godawful savor in our regular meat for the rest of the trip. Someday, Lloyd, I swear I'm going to honor your kindly intentions by staging another Indian-style pit barbecue—but not, I think, using fir-boughs, and certainly not featuring bear-cub tenderloins!

III

LEST I GIVE THE IMPRESSION that our journey around Mt. Jefferson was dominated by such mishaps involving domestic and wild animals, I need to convey somehow the everyday delights of the trip, the abiding warp of our experience of it, so to speak, on which these mishaps were only the colorful weft.

The cook-out at Table Lake excepted, we ate prodigiously and well—oatmeal, scrambled eggs and bacon, and pancakes or biscuits every morning; Spam, tuna, or peanut butter sandwiches for lunch; and the suppers … ! They were all sumptuous, but what I recall most fondly were the delicious "dough-gods" Dad and Lloyd made, a soda-rising camp bread they'd learned to make from John Campbell. You mixed up the ingredients right in the flour sack; what came out as dough was magically just what you needed. Then you baked them with reflected heat in a big frying-pan, tilted just so. Has the holy art of making dough-gods vanished with the generations? Certainly I don't know how.

When we were staying at Grizzly Flats, we were able to pick huckleberries, and I suppose the culinary high point of the whole trip was Dad's huckleberry dumplings, a whole meal unto themselves, if you were so lucky. I remember acutely envying Jim one night on the score of these soggy purple delicacies. He'd ridden back over Grizzly Mountain to fish at Pamelia Lake, and returned very late, well after dark, because of dense fog. He was duly scolded, and then—because most of our supper had been put away—he was allowed to eat up most of the rest of the huckleberry dumplings. He hadn't brought home any fish, either.

Day after usually cloudless day, we traveled through incredible alpine scenery; *this,* Mom and Thelma told each other, was why we'd come. The likelihood of a sudden new and breathtaking view of the mountain we thought we knew at home—so close you could hear its rock-falls, and feel its chilly breath—-drew us onward, even we three boys, all of us at an age when the sublime doesn't much register, at least not outwardly. And in the foreground, always the profusion of alpine wildflowers: Indian paintbrush of many hues, shooting stars, buttercups, sedums of every size and color, cascade lilies. Mom had brought one roll of newfangled Kodak color film to shoot, experimentally, and quickly used it up on the flowers.

Not that we just wafted along the trail, transported like Romantic poets from inspiration to inspiration. Our caravan of eight riders and thirteen animals (plus those outriders, the dogs) probably covered, at any one interval, a hundred yards of trail, from Dad and Lloyd in front, to Mom and me at the rear. From the mountain's perspective, we must have looked like a Chinese parade-dragon of many feet, inching along in our own dust. And stopping a lot; it seemed like we were *always* stopping, to deal with Geranium or one of the mules, or for the trailbosses to confer on our route, and maybe to ride ahead to look for signs of the trail we were supposed to be following. My mother took to speaking not unsarcastically of "these *mythical* trails." I'd never heard the word before, and it's still fixed in my mind that where there's a myth, there must be a trail. …

Whether over a discernable or a "conceptual" route, our way, as determined by Dad and Lloyd, lay over some pretty hair-raising terrain, where one's appreciation of the scenery being traversed tended to pucker down to a strict view of the horse's front feet, or just the saddle-horn. Even in mid-August, we had to slip and slither over huge snowbanks blocking the trail (if there was one); and we inched our way down many a precipitous scree-slope, the horses half-sitting down and sliding. Perhaps the scariest passage of all came one morning in crossing in rapid succession the "whitewater" creeks that flow directly out of the melting glaciers on Jefferson's west side. There were signs that warned DO NOT ATTEMPT TO CROSS AFTER 10 A.M., and although we were a little earlier than that, we could hear, as we prepared to cross, big rocks being rolled along in the violent milky current.

One of my annoyances with little Tommy was that, at such a moment but in truth at any time, he might be riding backwards on his colt, or standing up on her back like a circus performer. The fact of the matter, in case you haven't guessed it already, was that I was not an eager or confident horseman, despite the horseback "roadwork" Dad put Mom and me through to get us ready for the trip. I was not of a mind to openly enjoy myself on the trail; my interests lay distinctly elsewhere, in building and flying model planes, and reading. I went off and left aeronautical projects with ill-disguised reluctance; limited like all of us as to personal effects for the trip, I brought (besides my camera) a heavy book on model airplane theory, an "X-Acto" modeling knife, some balsa wood, and a tube of model glue. So while Tom was cavorting on the back of his pony, I was probably making like a caricature of the old-time Methodist circuit rider, ambling along apparently oblivious to everything but the book I was reading, or the airplane parts I was trying to glue together in the saddle. My parents did their best to ignore such perverse behavior, but it baffled Lloyd, bless him. "Jerry doesn't need to go off on a vacation like this," he was heard to say to no one in particular; "all he needs is to be taken to a library!"

But who can tell what a child is actually making of an experience like ours in 1949? I must have seemed, at the time, insufferably disaffected, and I regret the extent to which I did not let myself revel in the alpine paradise we daily traveled through, or for that matter fully share in the good fellowship of our company. But on the other hand, something of all this must have registered in the little snob reading his book in the saddle, for by the time I was eighteen I was mad for these mountains (though not on horseback), hiking and climbing in them with a kind of driven Wordsworthian passion. It's a passion from which I hope never to recover, and I'm grateful for the way it all began for me, on and off those "mythical" trails, back in August 1949.

IV

QUITE A FEW SUMMERS LATER, conscious of being at the edge of marriage, graduate school, and a career that would probably take me far from the mountains of central Oregon, I am hiking with a friend on the southern approaches to Mt. Jefferson. When we come within sight of the lovely meadows around Table Lake, I remember our bear-barbecue adventure there, years before. While my friend is fixing lunch at the lake, I wander off to see if I can find our old campsite. After the erasures of many winters, I can't be sure—until I spy, at the edge of the timber, what looks for all the world like a sunken, unmarked grave, the soil still appearing shoveled and bare of grass. For sure, it is our old barbecue pit. I stand there beside it for a long while, remembering all I can remember of that day, and those good people who shared it with me; and then I walk out of the shadows and on to the lakeshore, where I can see the whole changeless pyramid of Mt. Jefferson, without even looking for it.

Four

THE KILN

OUR BEST TRAVEL WRITERS CAN HOLD FORTH ALL DAY on the "mystique" of a big country like central Oregon, meaning, I suppose, the impact of its obvious natural features—mountains, canyons, rivers, forests, deserts—on natives and visitors. But to my mind, the real mystique here or anywhere is hidden away in stories of what might be (rather too grandly) called "mysteries of the land"—modest tales of unexplained, "never-seen-again" local wonders that come to occupy the minds of homefolks and serious visitors with obsessive force.

Any landscape, to those who love it, is full of lost treasures and marvels, not just glints of gold nuggets in a dry streambed, but more typically furtive hints of strange convergences of natural and human history, just waiting out there to be rediscovered. "Someone once saw something peculiar back in there, and you know, if it's still there we might be able to find traces of it, after all these years. ..."

In some storied regions like the Superstition Mountains or the Catskills, the storying process has long since taken on a life of its own, tales and speculations feeding on each other, almost disconnected from the distinctive Arizona or New York landforms and climates of their settings. But in central Oregon, the mysteries of the land remain more scattered, more elusive, less published—and therefore maybe more expressive of our final mystery: the land's elemental grip on the people who have moved across it, from Indian times onward, and given it voice.

I seem to have grown up listening to or overhearing tales of local wonders, mostly from hard-headed farmers and ranchers, too, not yarn-spinners, and therefore all the more compelling as pretexts to wild goose chases across the countryside. Is there anything more captivating than the prospect of setting out in search of reported marvels in a familiar landscape? For this appetite and affliction I am indebted to many elders, but especially to my maternal grandfather, Joe Mendenhall; my father, A. S. Ramsey; two of my uncles, Max Mendenhall and Cecil C. Moore; and our neighbor, John Campbell. They covered a lot of central Oregon history between them, these old-timers; but as flattering as it is to think that they told me stories because they thought I would be an appreciative and careful custodian, I also suspect that they mischievously enjoyed pushing my imaginative buttons, especially in later years when they knew it would take very little button pushing to send me questing out across the backcountry.

Maybe, some of the time, they were parcelling out their wonder-tales in the same playful spirit that leads Conan Doyle's Doctor Watson to tantalize his readers with allusions to not-yet-recorded Sherlock Holmes adventures—the singular affair of the aluminium crutch, for example, and the case of the Giant Rat of Sumatra, and other episodes for which, the Doctor hints darkly, "the world is not yet prepared." What reader can resist such fictive tickling of his or her imagination—but the stories I heard from my elders were all the more irresistible because they did not seem to be fictive, pointing instead to real, maybe confirmable prodigies, in settings I knew and loved as home ground.

What kinds of stories am I talking about? Here is a sampler from a list I'm still working on:

• An adult student of a teacher I know told him (and the teacher told me) that once, when he was logging below the east slopes of Olallie Butte, north of Mt. Jefferson, he found a gigantic arrow marked out in piled rocks on a steep open hillside. The logger-student didn't say which direction the arrow pointed. ...

• My grandfather Mendenhall claimed that ladybug beetles used to swarm all over the summit of Gray Butte on a certain day in spring, covering the rocks inches deep. He wasn't sure of the exact date, but thought it was in early April, and always on the same day!

• According to a "Looking Backward" column in the *Madras Pioneer*, in 1913 a Madras man, out hunting in the Willow Creek drainage southeast of town after an early snowfall, noticed that a patch of snow on a nearby rocky hillside had melted, exposing the ground. At the site, he found a strong current of warm air blowing out of a crack in the rocks, melting the snow. ...

• As a young buck, my grandfather's brother Walt Mendenhall once rode with some Yamhill County friends over the mountains and into the High Desert in search of gold—nominally the Lost Blue Bucket nugget site, but no doubt any treasure would do. They found nothing, but on the way back, near the head of the Metolius River, an older member of the party reminisced about his days as a militiaman at nearby Camp Polk during Indian troubles in 1865-66. Seems his company had lugged a brass cannon to the camp as part of their military equipment, and when the

Indian threats subsided and they were free to go back home to the Willamette Valley, they buried the cannon somewhere on the Camp Polk site. No one knows exactly where. Uncle Walt passed this bit of lore on to his nephew Max Mendenhall, who passed it on to *his* nephews. ...

• John Campbell once recalled venturing down into the deep jungly draw below Cabot Lake, south of Mt. Jefferson, in search of some strayed pack-horses. In a thicket alongside Cabot Creek, he stumbled on a small log cabin, well made but obviously very old, with no doors, and only a small window-sized opening high up on one wall. "I had too much ground to cover to look it over right then, so I told myself I would come back later and investigate it, but you know, I never did. ..."

And so on, and on—surely enough leads for a lifetime of wild goose expeditions into the heart of the country, and you're welcome to them! You will notice, however, that if it's precious metals that quickens your pulse and dilates your imagination, they're only incidental on this sample list—and tales of Bigfoot encounters and UFO sightings don't figure at all. The land-mystique or aura I'm talking about here is made up of stories altogether less vulgarly sensational, and now I want to tell the tale of a reported wonder that was actually tracked down and verified "in the field." The gist of it turns out to be an interesting bit of central Oregon's commercial and technological history; the magic was in the finding, and trying to understand, what had been lost for nearly a century.

SOME TIME AFTER WE BOUGHT TOM POWER'S PLACE in the hills east of Hay Creek Ranch and renamed it "The Sky Ranch," my dad went deer hunting in the Awbrey Butte country a few miles southwest of the place. Just below the crest of a ridge, facing south, he came upon an odd thicket of second-growth junipers, and in the center of the thicket he saw something remarkable. It was a stone-and-masonry structure, shaped, he said, like a pyramid with the top cut off, as high as the roof of a one-story house, with four odd window-like holes in its downhill side. There was no sign of occupation or activity around it. In subsequent hunting trips through that country, he showed it to a few friends and relatives, including John Campbell, and the general consensus was that it was some sort of *kiln*. But built for what purpose, and by whom, and when, nobody knew. All agreed that whatever it was, it was an outlandish thing; nothing like it in the territory!

When he told me the story years later, in the early 1970s, my dad was already past hiking over rough country, and he died before I could get him to locate the site on a map. But no matter—I had his usual sharp eyewitness account to go on: "Just below the crest of an east-west-running ridge, heading south, in a juniper thicket—and when you're there, you can look south across the draw and see the summit of Awbrey Butte."

But searching for something in the imagination and searching for it on both feet over the land (in this case, hilly, heavily forested, and brushy) are literally worlds apart, and although I made repeated forays into that lonely upland country alone or with willing or coerced family, and tried to be systematic by dividing the area into sectors and sweeping each one in turn, we found nothing. In western Ireland they have a mocking expression—"Send the Fool forward!"—and after peering into many a hillside thicket and finding nothing but more trees, I was beginning to feel like the Fool, unforwarded. *Which* east-west ridge, in a landscape resembling a washboard, did my father mean?

The fact is that, by the time the kiln was discovered, I'd given up on ever finding it (without admitting to myself that I had). A logger who had recently logged our place, and heard the story of the search, went on to do some logging in the Awbrey Creek drainage, and one of his fallers simply walked right up on the kiln, and told his boss, who told us, and drew us a map. Away we went.

My dad and his friends had not exaggerated: it *was* something truly outlandish, even stranger in actual view than in the imagination, so out of place on its hillside of juniper and jackpine, with nothing else human-made in sight, that it might have been dropped out of one of those chariots of the gods. It was, as reported, a truncated four-sided sharp-edged stone pyramid with a rough cement finish; about ten feet wide at the base, and eleven feet tall on its downhill side. And it was hollow, with walls over a foot thick. The "windows" my father spoke of, four of them, penetrated from the south face into the interior cavity: one at the base, like the hearth-opening of a fireplace; two just above, at either corner; and centered further up, a narrow slot that angled up into the interior.

I'd never seen a kiln before, except in books, but if this thing wasn't some sort of megalithic tomb or extraterrestial monument, it *did* look kiln-like. And in the gully running up the hillside behind the structure, we found telltale chunks of a dense milky-whitish rock—"calcite," calcium carbonate, the basic ore from which lime for mortar is "cooked," as in a kiln! The gully was actually an excavation following a vein of calcite a hundred and fifty feet or so up and into the hillside; from the looks of it, it had been worked extensively until the vein petered out. Fragments of timbers in the gully and atop the kiln suggested that there had been some sort of ramp or tramway from the former to the latter, whereby the calcite ore could be trundled up and dumped into the "flue" of the kiln.

If the otherworldliness of the thing was fading in the light of such discoveries, a new curiosity was emerging: here was real *technology* in a region where "hi-tech" still meant steel fence-posts you drove rather than wooden ones you dug holes for. So when, we were now asking, did the kiln operate, and how did it work? Maybe if we answered the technical questions, we could figure out who went to the considerable trouble of building it out here, and why.

As my father had reported, there were virtually no traces of the kiln's operation, other than some brittle fragments of leftover lime in the chamber that had been rained on and solidified into what appeared to be cement; and the surrounding thicket of runty, second-growth junipers, evidence that the original first-growth trees had been cut down for fuel. The fact that there were no stumps to be found suggested that the original trees had been cut a good long time ago, long enough for the stumps to rot away completely, even in this parched climate. I began to suppose a date around the turn of the century, and that guess became more plausible when we discovered a mature juniper that had grown up through what appeared to be the iron hoop of a small wooden keg, of the sort that was used to hold black powder in the days before the railroads came into central Oregon, 1909-11.

Otherwise, we found no "occupational" traces at the site, of the usual kind—no rusty cans, bottles, jars, broken tools. It was time to shift to the indoor phase of our quest, and look for records and documents.

First, what sort of limekiln was this? In *A Practical Treatise on Lime, Hydraulic Cements, and Mortars*, by Q. A. Gillmore, published in 1863 as part of what appears to be a series of practical guides to do-it-yourself engineering, we learned that our specimen would have been called an *intermittent* kiln, a design once in widespread use across America, especially in limestone-rich states like Indiana. Unlike its hi-tech cousin the *perpetual* or continuous kiln, which usually burned coal and produced lime continuously and efficiently, the intermittent model burned wood, was not very efficient, but could turn out a decent amount of lime in three or four days and nights of continuous burning, and then would be shut down and allowed to cool off and be emptied, before being loaded up with ore and wood and fired up again, at need.

> For burning common lime, the simplest form of kiln in common use in Europe (and, with some slight modifications, in the United States) is [the intermittent kiln], in which wood is used for fuel. This kiln is circular in horizontal section [not true of our kiln] and is generally constructed of rough-hammered limestone without mortar [likewise not the case here]. It is usually located on the side of a hill, so that the top is accessible for charging the kiln, and the bottom for supplying the fuel, and drawing out the burnt lime. The largest pieces of the stone to be burned are first selected and formed into an arch [at the base of the flue, just above the burning area]. Above this arch, the kiln is filled by throwing the stone in loosely from the top, taking the largest first, and the smaller pieces afterward. …

Gillmore goes on to urge caution in starting the fire under the load of calcite:

> The heat should be raised gradually to the required degree [elsewhere he says "red-hot"]. There is a controlling reason for this: a sudden elevation of temperature will cause a sudden explosion of the stones [in the arch of chockstones in the flue], and the moisture will be driven off with such force as to rupture them in many cases. As the stones are of irregular shape and unconnected with mortar of any kind, the consequence might be a downfall of the entire contents of the kiln, and of course an interruption of the burning. Moreover, a too sudden elevation of temperature might cause many of the stones to break up into small pieces, and thereby seriously choke the draught, without injuring the arch.

Gillmore also notes that, to do its job, an intermittent kiln needs to be kept burning day and night for several days, and he estimates that about four cords of wood will be required for a typical kiln of this type and size to burn its charge of limestone. Dry figures, but now a picture of the truly labor-intensive operation of our Awbrey Butte kiln began to clarify. Having labored mightily to build the thing, hauling and dressing and mortaring stones on a dry hillside (Awbrey Creek is more than a quarter-mile below), the crew would then have begun to excavate the calcite vein, probably using black powder and picks. The next step would be to build the crucial arch or, more correctly, dome of chockstones in the flue, as described by Gillmore—this would be work both heavy and delicate. I know: I tried my hand at it, and failed utterly—clearly, building it would take *several* pairs of expert, well-coordinated hands, holding the chunks in place until they would wedge each other up against gravity.

Then, with the dome complete and the flue plugged, the whole upper "chimney" of the kiln would be filled with fragments of calcite, while other members of the crew might be cutting trees for fuel, chopping them into short lengths to fit, and carefully "laying the fire" in the hearth through the main opening at the base of the kiln. A cord of wood is reckoned as a pile four feet by four by eight; the four cords required for a complete burning in a typical intermittent kiln, according to Gillmore, would be an impressive piece of wood-chopping. Igniting the fire would then focus the work detail on the single intense task of feeding and regulating it nonstop for three or four days and nights, until the whole load of calcite had been transformed into quicklime.

After the kiln had cooled off, its contents would be extracted through the three large openings in front (the topmost upward-slanting hole must have been for draft) and placed in barrels, either directly, if the lime came out in powder form, or, if it was lumpy, after the lumps had been mashed or ground into powder. Then a long haul in wagons to the building site—where?—and then a final crucial and arduous step: mixing or "slaking" the lime with water to make a heavy paste, which would need to season for a spell, before mixing it with fine sand (one part lime, two-and-one-half parts sand) to make *mortar.* Then the bricklaying or stonemasonry could at last begin.

Putting all this labor into chemical shorthand makes a pretty illustration of technology at work. Heating calcite ($CaCO_3$) drives off the carbon dioxide, leaving CaO, quicklime; mixing CaO with water allows it to reabsorb CO_2 from the air, as the water evaporates, producing (along with the generation of a lot of heat) calcium hydroxide, $Ca(OH)_2$: voilà, the basis of mortar, the only stuff to join bricks or stones together! It's doubtful that the crew that operated our hillside kiln knew the chemical basis of these transformations, but understanding the chemistry makes their practical knowhow all the more impressive. Thinking of my own backyard struggles at masonry involving "Sakrete" or "Redi-Mix" from a truck, I wondered if anybody in these parts today would have the savvy to "burn lime" and make mortar this way from scratch.

I also wondered what it must have been like, attending one of the marathon burning sessions—probably camping down on Awbrey Creek and trudging up to the kiln site for, say, an all-night shift, feeling the blistering heat of the thing before you reached it, watching the weird shadows cast by the glare of its innards on the surrounding trees, maybe worrying about sparks setting off a forest fire as you fed it more wood from the dwindling pile. ...

But now it was time to move from questions of how, to questions of *why?* We'd rediscovered a spectacular example of the technological self-sufficiency of our central Oregon forebears, what appears to have been the only working lime kiln in this region—but what was its purpose? How was all that work and expertise on a remote hillside going to meet a need and make somebody—the boss, the crew—some money?

Working on the assumption that our kiln was built and operated before the advent of railroads in this country, I looked into freighting costs before and after the Oregon Trunk and Union Pacific came in. In the years before 1912, when mule skinners like my great-grandfather Julius McCoin made a living freighting goods to Prineville and other communities from the Columbia Southern railhead at Shaniko and before 1900, all the way from The Dalles, the cost of shipping heavy bulk stuff like cement and plaster would have been prohibitive—on the order of two cents a pound just from Shaniko to Madras. In terms of the total cost of delivered goods: by freight wagon, a barrel of lime cost around seven dollars and fifty cents, a barrel of ready-to-use Portland cement cost fifteen dollars; by railroad, these prices fell to two dollars and seventy-five cents for lime and four dollars and a quarter for cement—a graphic illustration of the huge economic impact of the railroads in the opening-up of a new region like this one. Not just the furnishing of houses and buildings but the the basic elements of the buildings themselves, suddenly became affordable to "import."

For our kiln and its operators, such figures seem to confirm a date before the railroads, when a source of locally produced lime could surely expect to outbid imported stuff. But where, in central Oregon before 1912, would there have been enough need for mortar to justify such an elaborate operation? I was stumped: we had the supply side of our mystery pretty well figured out, but where was the demand? In a country where locally milled Ponderosa pine and Douglas fir lumber was plentiful and cheap from the 1890s on, almost all public and private buildings were being constructed of wood, at least above ground-level.

I didn't have long to dither. In December 1989 something happened in Prineville that made headlines throughout the Northwest, and fortuitously, once I heard the news, seemed to solve the mystery of our kiln's purpose. It was reported that the massive clock tower of the historic Crook County Courthouse was leaning ominously and was in imminent danger of crashing down through the third-floor court-chambers; the whole building was evacuated and closed, at least until drastic structural repairs could be attempted. Happily, they were successful and the building was eventually re-opened, but at the time, Prineville's very bad news served to remind me of what I should have thought of when we first found the kiln. Namely, that the construction of what was for many years central Oregon's biggest stone building (three stories tall, with a massive basalt foundation, steps, and vault, made of locally quarried basalt) would be reason enough in itself to set up a local source of lime for mortar. The courthouse was built in 1907-09, exactly in our hypothetical time frame for the Awbrey Butte kiln, and right in the middle of a remarkable stone-building boom in Prineville that also gave the town a new high school (1904-05), the First National Bank building (1906), the Masonic Hall (1909), and the Crook County Bank building, now the Bowman Museum (1910). According to an article in the *Central Oregon Journal* for February 3, 1905, "the discovery of a quarry of excellent building-stone just west of the city has apparently formed the nucleus from which will spring several stone and brick buildings." With local stone inexpensively available, why not lime, mortar, and cement, too, if a local source could be found—especially for a project as big and costly as the new courthouse?

One of the fascinations of historical research, whether on a grand or a local scale, is the possibility that one thread of inquiry will, if followed out, eventually intersect with other seemingly unrelated threads, until a whole warp-and-woof historical pattern is revealed. So here, in the possible connection of the kiln to the Courthouse, although I must confess that my first response to the connection was, "Oh my God— the courthouse is collapsing because it was built with substandard mortar from our kiln!" Not so; it's been determined that the leaning clock tower was badly engineered, in jeopardy from the start, but the story of *that* circumstance significantly connects both with the small fact of the kiln itself and with a major episode in the political history of the whole region.

At the turn of the twentieth century, Prineville was still the undisputed county seat and center of government of a vast swatch of country called Crook County, including all of what is now Crook, Deschutes, and Jefferson counties—an area about the size of Massachusetts, reaching from the Mutton Mountains south to Hampton Butte in the High Desert, and from the Cascade crest east all the way to Suplee. But by the middle of that first decade, intensive homesteading and settlement in the Deschutes River country to the west led to demands that either the county seat be relocated to a more central place, or one or even two new counties be formed out of Crook's northwest and southwest territories. Agitation for the latter measure became especially strong in Bend, an upstart mill-town on the upper Deschutes. The insurgent "Westsiders" were led by A. M. Drake, director of the Pilot Butte Development Company and one of the founders of Bend.

The response in Prineville to this agitation seems to have been to lay plans for building a sumptuous new county courthouse, thereby consolidating the town's lock on the county seat. When these plans were revealed in 1905, Bend and other outlying communities united in protest, demanding that as long as they had to be part of Crook County, the tax moneys earmarked for the new courthouse should be spent instead on roads and other public works in their neglected districts. An injunction blocking construction on the basis of existing contracts was issued.

Prineville's reaction was to reject the original bids for the project, from contractors in Salem and Portland, and to sign a new contract, based on a much lower bid ($48,500) from the Prineville firm of Wright and McNeely. Civic pride, stirred up by the Westside opposition (which was claiming that the courthouse would really cost taxpayers over seventy-five thousand dollars), yielded a handsome fund of $6,400 in private subscriptions, money for the job that would not have to come out of taxes. (Several years later, however, after the courthouse was completed, the county clerk was still trying to get subscribers to make good on their civic promises.)

But meanwhile, the work was begun posthaste. The massive basalt blocks were blasted and hammered out of the new quarry on the rimrock southwest of town, and on March 21, 1907, the *Central Oregon Journal* reported that "stone is in the ground for the basement work."— It must have been a mild March, because Wright and McNeely's contract specified that "No stone is to be laid during freezing weather and no mortar is to be used that has been frozen."

The work on the foundation and the steps went forward through 1907, but in January 1908 came very bad news: Wright and McNeely indicated that they would be unable to carry out their contract to finish the upper stories of the building, and were declared "in default." McNeely told the court that his partner, Wright, had abruptly left the company, leaving it with no expertise in woodwork and plumbing—but one wonders if the root cause of their collapse was that they had drastically underbid the job in the first place. Whatever the case, with opposition continuing from the Westsiders, the new Crook County Courthouse-to-be stood idle, its foundations supporting nothing, and its massive steps leading nowhere.

Enter, to the rescue, an improbable and endearing local character named Jack Shipp. Shipp's credentials for becoming contractor of central Oregon's first large stone building were off-center, to say the least. Born in Lancastershire, England, he had come to Portland with his family as a boy, and been apprenticed to a cake decorator, before setting up in business himself as a bicycle repairman. After landing in Prineville around 1900 (he came by bicycle), he opened a bike shop, built a small planing-mill and several private houses, and in 1904 served as "architect" of the new Crook County High School. Still, even for someone so versatile and self-confident, taking on the completion of an unfinished and politically embattled courthouse was a very tall order indeed—but the work had to go forward without delay against the threat of new Westside challenges and injunctions, and it did, with Shipp fearlessly in charge. A Portland stonemasonry firm, Phillips and Douglass, was brought in to finish the masonry work.

When the courthouse was completed in May 1909, Shipp and his team had done the job for an incredibly low cost of $48,591! Only the near-collapse of the clock-tower eighty years later suggests that he may well have been in over his head as a contractor, on some points of structural engineering at least. In the central Oregon of those days, with so much to be done, people met necessity and opportunity head-on, and often combined them with impressive entrepreneurial moxie. Everybody agreed (at least in Prineville): Jack Shipp was the man. Before he had finished the building and it opened in May 1909, he had contributed a flagpole to it, and also done the initial landscaping at his own expense! No wonder that the county court declared "its thanks and appreciation to contractor Jno. B. Shipp, not only for his strict and careful compliance with the letter and intent of the plans and specifications of the

Courthouse, but also for upwards of $370 worth of extra work and materials [contributed] at no cost to the County."

So Prineville got a fine new stone courthouse (and soon after, as I've said, two new stone bank buildings and a Masonic hall), but nonetheless, the agitation to divide the county grew unchecked, spurred on by the completion of the railroad through the communities of Madras, Redmond, and Bend (bypassing Prineville); and in the next decade, two new counties were in fact carved out of Crook County, Jefferson in 1915 and Deschutes in 1916.

What was our little kiln doing during all this activity? No doubt busy cooking lime for all it was worth, almost certainly for the other stone buildings as well as the courthouse, meaning an intermittent run from 1904 to 1910—just before the advent of cheap railroad freight would have put it out of business. I recently found, on a another hillside a mile or so from the site, evidence of another calcite-vein excavation, but without a kiln. Presumably, when the original vein was used up, our kiln was kept going with ore carted from this second supply.

Amusingly, a modern map shows that the presumed source of the lime and mortar that may have built Crook County's courthouse is located just inside the southern boundary of what became, in a few years, Jefferson County. The route from here to downtown Prineville is obvious: down and across Awbrey Creek, up and around the flank of Awbrey Butte, down to the historic "A-Y" road, and so on down Allen and then McKay creeks to Prineville—maybe twenty miles on roads that existed then.

And who were our lime-cooking operators? A search through courthouse records turned up no contracts, only this tantalizing 1907 entry in the county commissioners' journal: "Mortar to be mixed and stocked at least 12 days before using, and to be of such proportions as may be designated by the Supt. (not to exceed six bbl. of mortar to one bbl. of lime.)" What this means, pretty conclusively, is that quicklime as from our kiln was to be used on the job, not Portland cement or "ready-mix": quicklime needs to be slaked with water, remember, and then mixed with sand to make mortar. But who provided the quicklime?

Playing a hunch, I searched through mineral-claim records for Crook County, the hunch being that a mining claim might be on file, identifying our lime-cookers or at least their sponsors. The records reveal that there *was* a fever of mining speculation in the area about this time, with claims entered for gold, silver, gypsum, oil, natural gas, even for a very poor quality soft coal. But even when a claim specified a particular mineral, say silver, it could serve as the basis for removal of other minerals as well, as in a frequent phrase in these records: "claiming all surface rights, privileges, and minerals." Hence it appeared unlikely that I could locate the claim that was actually the basis of our lime-cooking operation.

Or so it seemed, until research on another central Oregon topic led me quite by accident to a discovery that directly challenged my working theory about the Awbrey Butte kiln and its purpose. A *Madras Pioneer* article of June 1, 1911, headlined "Enormous Dike of Almost Pure Lime," reported that a man named Cavaney and several partners had recently discovered an extensive deposit of limestone (over one hundred acres!) located about four miles south of Hay Creek Ranch headquarters, "near the Elkins Place." Cavaney and his associates declared that the deposit, which they named "Spar King," "bids fair to become one of the most valuable lime properties on the Pacific Coast if not the United States," and noted that they were building a kiln below the "ledge" of ore, and that the kiln would be of "the continuous type, in which the unburned rock is put in at the top, and the finished rock drawn out from the bottom, there being no necessity for the fires ever to go out." The report concludes: "The owners have in view the construction of a warehouse in Madras and expect to sack the rock from the kiln and haul it to the warehouse where it will be put in barrels and probably hydrated and further prepared for marketing." Clearly they intended to ship their product over the Oregon Trunk railroad, which had only recently reached Madras, on February 15.

So was this, after all, the real story behind our kiln—the work of Madras entrepreneurs, and unrelated to Prineville's heroic building boom, coming several years afterward?

Armed with the date of the *Pioneer* article, I went back to the Crook County Courthouse and checked the county mining-claim records again, this time for 1911. Sure enough, in a multiple entry dated May 18, 1911, W. M. Cavaney, W. G. McCoy, and J. H. Barkley entered claims for "Lime Spar," "Spar King," and four other sites. Only for "Lime Spar" did they specify the mineral they were after; the other claims were unspecific. My hope to compare the legal description of their lime claim, and the actual legal location of the Awbrey Butte kiln, and thus either confirm or refute this new possibility, came to nothing because mining claims did not require legal descriptions in those days. Instead, Cavaney and his mates merely noted that "Lime Spar" was about six miles southeast of Hay Creek Ranch. The other five claims appear to have been contiguous with "Lime Spar," apparently running in a jagged swath varying in width from three to seven hundred feet, from somewhere about five miles southeast of Hay Creek to about six and one-half miles. They refer to "monuments," "center stakes," "location posts," and so on, but it's hard to see how such markers would have served much purpose in such rough and brushy country, even then. No wonder miners were always accusing each other of "jumping claims."

Notice that the newspaper article locates "Spar King" (apparently they meant "Lime Spar"?) about *four* miles *south* of Hay Creek headquarters, "near the Elkins Place," whereas in the claim it's *six* miles *southeast*. Six miles would bring you to within a mile or two of the Awbrey Butte kiln site, depending of course on what angle of "southeast" you took, and indeed the old Elkins place (now part of Hay Creek) is maybe two miles distant. But such coordinates are in truth much too vague to allow us to settle the issue on their merits alone.

What is *not* vague, and strongly suggests that Cavaney's 1911 claim is *not* the basis of the Awbrey Butte kiln, is that he and his partners told the *Pioneer* that they were building a kiln "of the continuous type" with "no necessity for the fires ever to go out," and that they clearly meant for their enterprise to become a sizeable commercial venture, requiring a warehouse, facilities for mixing, hydrating, and packing, and railroad distribution. Now by all accounts, "continuous" or "perpetual" kilns were massive, sophisticated installations, with firebrick linings, air-chambers, iron-gratings, baffles, etc., and usually involving the use of coal as fuel. As we've seen, the Awbrey kiln is on the contrary a classic example of the old-time "intermittent" kind, needing to be loaded with ore and fuel between every burning, and incapable both in efficiency of burning and in capacity of supporting the kind of business venture that Cavaney and Co. apparently had in mind. Likewise, the calcite vein (not a "ledge") that supplied the Awbrey kiln until the ore ran out was clearly nothing like the "enormous dike" of Cavaney's newspaper report.

From such evidence, then, I conclude that the "Lime Spar" claim, wherever it was and whatever happened to it, is not to be identified with our little kiln above Awbrey Creek. Calcite outcroppings are in fact common enough all through that country, and it's entirely possible that Cavaney and his partners made their claims somewhere thereabouts, possibly further southwest in the draws and canyons running towards Grizzly Mountain. I've found no records of their building or operating a warehouse in Madras after 1911; but maybe their massive "continuous" kiln was actually built, and still stands somewhere out in that scrubby, unsettled country, waiting to be found. More likely it was constructed only in the pages of the *Pioneer*.

But enough time spent on this unexpected detour (and new mystery); let's return to the Awbrey kiln, and our original working hypothesis that it was built and operated to support Prineville's stone-building boom, notably the construction of the courthouse. Again, who was in charge? Could it have been set up and operated by one of the stonemasonry subcontractors, the Portland firm of Phillips and Douglass or its unrecorded predecessor, which presumably also operated the stone-quarry for the project? Very likely, given the strong cost-saving incentives Jack Shipp and the town fathers had their contractors working under—but again no confirming records have been found. Certainly the quality of the workmanship on the kiln itself suggests that it was done by the kind of skilled workmen—possibly European artisans?—that an urban company like Phillips and Douglass would employ. But, lacking the records of that long-dissolved firm, who knows?

Who knows indeed? Maybe, instead of a reputable masonry contractor and his team of professionals, our kiln (like so much else in this country) was the creation of someone like Jack Shipp, another recent arrival in the territory from Elsewhere who brought with him useful knowledge and unbounded self-confidence, and saw a local need that could become his opportunity to make good money with little investment beyond hard work. So in this particular phase of his career of such bold ventures, our conjectural freelance kilnsman might have located a good calcite source up in the hills, gathered his crew, possibly consulted a manual like Gillmore's, and gone to work, learning as he went, eventually selling lime at a good profit to the mighty contractors in Prineville. It's a nice scenario: implausible, you say, but don't forget Jack Shipp himself, cake decorator, bicycle mechanic, and self-made master builder.

At any rate, it's pleasant that all such speculation can come home, if not to final verification, at least to the sturdy reality of those fine old stone buildings in Prineville, their foundations and walls expertly hewn and dressed out of native rimrock, and as far as I know, mortared together with homemade cement from our improbable lime-kiln on its lonely hillside in Jefferson County, still looking out over Awbrey Butte, towards the county seat of Crook.

And if you'd like to mount your own wild-goose chase through this country in search of Mr. Cavaney's "Lime Spar" claim and his continuous kiln, well, good luck, and please let me know what you find out there.

Five

OPAL CITY

❖

I HAVE COME ONCE AGAIN to the site of our family ghost town, "Opal City," knowing in advance that I won't find much of anything—but on this raw, overcast February day I find nothing, nothing at all. Even the black-on-white section signs on the switch-markers are gone. The Burlington Northern/Conrail tracks sweep relentlessly northwest and southeast to the horizons, with nothing here at this unmarked crossing to detain the visitor, or indicate to him that once, briefly, nearly a century ago, there was the purpose and possibility of a town here. Now even the railroad's splintery leavings, monuments of my childhood—the old water tower, the depot, the warehouse on the siding—are long gone, and the townsite itself lies erased under irrigated fields. To the north, my grandfather's homestead house stands vacant, derelict. All that's left of Opal City, I realize, is an untold story: and who can remember its episodes and details?

❖

I CALL IT "OUR FAMILY GHOST TOWN" not to claim ironic ownership, but rather to indicate that my mother's family, the Mendenhalls, were present and active at its birth, so to speak, and then, for the long remainder of the twentieth century, they were its unappointed custodians. They were "the Mendenhalls of Opal City."

Exactly one hundred years ago, as I write this, in spring 2000, my grandfather, Joe Mendenhall (then twenty-five and single), his older brother Walt (thirty-four and married, with two small children), and their parents Mordecai Michael, "Mike" (sixty-five), and Nancy Catherine (fifty-eight) were preparing to leave the family domains near Sheridan, in Yamhill County south of Portland, and take up homesteads on an unnamed sagebrush flat between Juniper Butte and the final bend of the Crooked River, in what was then the western reaches of Crook County.

Whether the two brothers came on ahead, as seems likely, followed in due course by their parents and Walt's family, or whether they all made the trip together, nobody remembers. Presumably they came by way of

Salem and then over the old Santiam wagon road and down from the mountains to Sisters and so on across the Deschutes River at Tetherow's Bridge and across Crooked River at Trail Crossing; what wagons and livestock, tools and furniture they brought with them across the mountains has been forgotten in family memory. But by 1901 they were bona fide central Oregon homesteaders, busy doing what had to be done to "prove up" on three adjoining 160-acre claims, laying out their fields, grubbing and burning sagebrush, and building dwellings. Joe was working part-time at Jack Dee's sawmill on Grizzly Mountain fifteen miles to the east (according to family tradition he sometimes *bicycled* back and forth), and very likely he took some of his wages in green lumber for the family's buildings.

And their little community on the south side of Juniper Butte, with the breathtaking vistas west and south to the Cascades skyline, soon acquired a name, "Yamhill Flat," as relatives and friends from that historic but hardscrabble county—Lamsons, Barbers, Ralstons and others—came over the mountains and took up homestead claims nearby. Many of these families, the Mendenhalls included, had already gone through one migration, from Jefferson County, Tennessee, to Oregon's north Willamette Valley, in the desperate years following the Civil War. Now here they were again, one generation later, trying their fortunes anew in a country that was much more raw and much less friendly to farming than the fertile valley land they'd come to in the sixties and seventies. Why were they homesteading again, east of the mountains?

No doubt each of the twenty or thirty families on Yamhill Flat had its own bundle of needs, aspirations, and reasons for coming there, but they were also loosely "clanned" together by family and neighborly ties going far back. In the case of the Mendenhalls, Walt seems to have been the chief instigator of the move, having scouted central Oregon out in the 1880s in the course of an over-the-mountains prospecting trip with Yamhill County friends. No doubt his tales about the dry, wide-open hinterlands found an eager listener in younger brother Joe, single and as the youngest of five sons not likely to inherit any Yamhill property.

As for their father and mother, already elderly by nineteenth-century standards, they must have wanted to see for themselves what their sons were getting into, and help them claim as much of the new land as possible by filing on a quarter-section of their own; the boys would do the work and eventually acquire the land. It was a common and entirely legal homesteading strategy in Oregon and elsewhere; my great-grandfather John Ramsey did the same for *his* son William on Agency Plains and then returned to Missouri, his pioneering done. For their part "Mike" and Nancy Mendenhall proved up and received title to their land, which they sold to Walt, and then promptly went home to Yamhill County, where Mike died soon after, in 1910, just as their corner of Yamhill Flat was being promoted as "Opal City." But our story is getting ahead of itself, as such stories will.

In those earliest years, the Mendenhall boys experimented with crops of wheat, oats, and barley, and their father discovered that the light dry soil would grow impressive vegetable crops, especially watermelons, if enough water could be diverted from household and livestock uses. Walt and Joe joined their neighbors in exploring the nearby Crooked River Gorge, fishing there in summer and trapping for mink and muskrat in winter, and hunting mule deer in the hills to the east. Up to a point subsistence was not difficult; you really could live off the land spring, summer, and fall. But the nearest stores and medical services were in Prineville, thirty miles to the east, and the nearest railroad terminus was in Shaniko, two days' hard travel to the north. More immediately challenging to everybody was the lack of *water*: it had to be hauled from springs up in the Grey Butte foothills several miles away, stored in barrels or cisterns, and used more than once wherever possible. A copious spring of pure water—known as "Opal Springs" because of the opaline pebbles polished in its outlet basin—gushed into the Crooked River a few miles northwest, but no one had figured out how to bring the water up out of the canyon, nearly five hundred vertical feet below the Flat. Drilling wells that deep was out of the question, at least for beginning homesteaders, or "entrymen," as they were called by the government.

A domestic water system would have to wait, while more pressing needs were addressed. A school was soon started, and a Grange. The two Mendenhall brothers were accomplished musicians, Joe on the fiddle and Walt on the banjo and the bones, and they were much in demand at dances and socials around the country. In the course of such "circulations," Joe began to court a tall, pretty girl from over on Grey Butte, Ella McCoin, an expert horsewoman, and pretty soon they were married. But Walt's wife Gertrude, already unwell when they moved to Yamhill Flat, did not thrive in the central Oregon climate, and she died in the winter of 1903. He never remarried.

It's hard to pin a precise date on the passage of a rumor, even a big one, but sometime around 1906 (the year my mother was born, the third of Joe and Ella's four children) the citizens of Yamhill Flat began to hear talk of the railroad coming through central Oregon—probably, it was said, right through their neck of the woods! This would not be a mere extension of the little "Columbia Southern" line, either, which had gotten as far into the country as Shaniko, making it briefly the jumping-off and shipping-out terminus for the interior, but something on a grand national scale, being planned (so the gossip ran) in the board rooms "Back East" of James J. Hill's Great Northern line, and E. H. Harriman's Union Pacific. Somehow, it was said, one or both of these giants of unrestrained capitalism were going to lay track up the lower Deschutes River canyon from its Columbia River mouth as far south as possible, and then across the rolling country south and west of the new town of Madras to the Crooked River Gorge, where an enormous bridge would have to be built, before the tracks could move on through the broad Deschutes River valley to the new town of Bend, at the northern edge of unlimited, mostly untapped timberlands.

Nothing much happened for a few years, it seems, except for much idle talk and expansive conjecturing about this theoretical route, until June 1908, when the news officially broke. Hill and his arch-rival Harriman were indeed planning to blast and hammer their lines in a mad race up the opposite sides of the Deschutes, Hill's "Oregon Trunk" on the west side, Harriman's "Deschutes Railroad" on the east, and damn the cost! The little green-lumber towns and settlements of central Oregon, including Yamhill Flat, were electrified by the news.

The only interior town *not* much caught up in railroad fever was, ironically, the county seat, Prineville, apparently too far to the east to figure in any Hill or Harriman route survey. The city fathers of Prineville, who had only recently started building a splendid new stone courthouse, and were fighting off mounting agitation from western Crook County factions for the creation of a separate new county, were understandably worried over the prospects of being bypassed by "the silver rails of commerce." Could a Prineville spur-line be built?

Prineville's anxieties notwithstanding, almost overnight, it seemed, the stage-lines from Shaniko into the country were overrun with a colorful assortment of impromptu would-be homesteaders, land and business speculators of every degree and shade of honesty, journalists sent out to report on the opening of this newest American frontier, and, as always, history's tumbleweeds, "along for the ride." Opportunity was suddenly in the air like sagebrush smoke over Yamhill Flat: for the settlers already "landed" there, for the visitors now streaming in, looking things over, smelling the heady scent of transient deals and quick profits. How to make the most of such manifold and magnificent opportunity?

At Yamhill Flat, geology offered one obvious main chance, in the form of the gorge of the Crooked River, three hundred fifty feet wide and deeper than that. It would clearly take an army-sized construction camp to build a bridge over the gorge, and where would the builders live, and how would their human needs be supplied, and by whom, during the estimated two years of their work? Well before the engineers and the workers arrived at the site (in the late summer of 1909), local entrepreneurs were planning ways of making themselves indispensable to the project—including one imaginative homesteader who announced that he intended to provide the bridge builders with a laundry service, using water to be winched up from Crooked River! Others, including the Mendenhall brothers, were thinking more practically, in terms of stores, saloons, feed and livery barns, and so on.

But these were all short-term schemes, and soon—in fall 1909—they were all subsumed in the ultimate formulation of opportunity for Yamhill Flat: the creation of a new town squarely in the way of the coming railroad, to be called "Opal City." No doubt local visionaries had already entertained some such scheme for their community, but inevitably it took outsiders and their capital to make the vision seem even briefly credible. In this case, the outsiders were a syndicate of Portland investors calling themselves the Opal City Land Company. Their spokesman and chief stockholder was a developer already well known in central Oregon, Joseph Houston. Other principals included William Morfitt, Clarence Gilbert, and Wilford Jones, all from Portland. The auspicious first announcement of the founding of Opal City appeared in the Prineville *Central Oregon Journal* in October 1909, and I quote from it at length here, to convey the force and flavor of the enterprise.

"OPAL CITY IS NAME OF NEW TOWNSITE"

Opal City is the name of a new townsite that is soon to be put on the market in Crook County. Joseph G. Houston,representing a Portland syndicate, has purchased of Walter Mendenhall his 160-acre homestead on Yamhill Flat, and the plat of the new city will be filed with the county clerk within the next few days. The land is on the line of both the Hill and Harriman surveys for the new

railroads, and is said by those familiar with the lay of
things to be one of the finest prospective townsites in
central Oregon. The price paid for the quarter section was
$4000. It is located on the south-east slope of Juniper
Butte above Opal Springs, hence the name Opal City.

Mr. Houston is the general manager of the Odin Falls
development corporation, and while this venture is not part
of the Odin Falls project, the promoters will reserve the
water, light, and power rights in the deeds of dedication,
and expect to supply these utilities from the plant on the
Deschutes. Mr. Houston is now in Prineville and is calling
for bids for the construction of the power dam at Odin
Falls. It is understood that County Commissioner Bayley
may take the contract for constructing the dam. ...

Another feature of the plan which will be of interest to
Prineville people is that a preliminary survey for an electric
railway line will soon be made from Opal City to
Prineville. The projected route skirts the base of Haystack
[Butte], runs north of Lamonta, and swings through the
gap below the oil well [a recent promotion that eventually
fizzled] on the slope of Grizzly Mountain, thence across
"Poverty Flat" to Prineville. Developments in this direction
will be closely watched by Prineville people.

It's an imaginative stretch to comprehend a time in America when
towns were being invented, platted, and "put on the market" to be sold
street by hypothetical street to eager would-be residents, but that's exactly
what was happening in 1909-10 in the forward wake of the central
Oregon railroad boom. As it happened, Opal City had a twin and rival:
on the same day, November 23, 1909, that the Crook County Court
met to consider its townsite application, they also considered one from
the Crook County Investment Corporation for the town of Hillman, to
be located south of the gorge about seven miles from Yamhill Flat. The
name "Hillman," it was widely understood, was coined to honor (and
flatter) James J. *Hill* and Edward Harri*man*. Both townsites were duly
approved for public sale by the court; it couldn't have hurt their chances
for approval that both applications included mention of plans to build a
spur railway line from their fair cities to Prineville. The already-hatched
townlets of Metolius and Redmond also were making noises about

providing a rail connection to Prineville. (In 1912, a confidence-man named H. H. Skewes blew into Metolius as a promoter of the Prineville line, sold worthless stocks, raised money for materials, courted and married the Widow Sparks, owner of the Sparks Hotel, and skipped town just as his scam began to unravel.) As it turned out, Prineville had to build its own spur-line in 1918, to this day the only municipally owned railroad in America, connecting with the Burlington Northern/Conrail line directly between Hillman (now Terrebonne) and Redmond.

Another townsite to be launched in that heady period was located in the Deschutes River canyon west of Agency Plains, near Madras. This was Vanora, the brainchild of a farmer-promoter named Ora Van Tassell, who unabashedly coined the town's name out of his own. By 1911, when the Oregon Trunk line came up the Deschutes Canyon, Vanora was waiting for it, with a store, a post office, a domestic water system, and a school, which my father attended for several years.

And six months after Opal City's birth announcements, rumors of yet another townsite promotion were reported in the Madras *Pioneer* of March 10, 1910. The *Pioneer*'s reporter did not seem especially impressed by what he'd heard: "Another new townsite is projected, it being located in the Opal Prairie district, about eight miles south of Madras, on the places formerly owned by Dee Swift and Fred Killingbeck, but now owned by J. C. Cockerham and William C. Barber."

"Opal Prairie" was once used to describe the country from Yamhill Flat north around the west flanks of Juniper Butte to what is now the town of Culver—and clearly, what this indifferent notice points to is the founding of Culver. Or, rather, the re-founding, because the town had been originally established some miles to the east, at the north edge of Haystack Butte, but in 1908-09, with railroad rumors flying, the town decided to move itself, lock, stock, and post office, to a new location at the edge of Opal Prairie, squarely in the projected path of the railroad. Joe Mendenhall's friend, Bill Barber (in years to come the father of World War Two ace Rex Barber, who shot down Admiral Yamamoto), was a major promoter of the deal, and generally reckoned as the father of New Culver.

By 1911, the relocating job was done, and Culver was in business again; unlike Opal City, Hillman, and Vanora, it had the distinct advantage of having been a town before, elsewhere. An April 6, 1911 article in the Redmond *Spokesman* notes that it already had these hallmarks of a real town: a commercial club, a volunteer fire department, a newspaper, and a brass band. By 1914, when Jefferson County was created out of Crook County, Culver was thriving, to the point that it served briefly as the seat of the new county, before—as Culverites will still tell you, indignantly—"Madras stole it away." But that is, as the saying goes, another story.

Was there maybe a hint of sharp practices, even fraudulence, in all this excitement over creating marketable townsites out of homesteads, in the path of the advancing railroads? The case of "Hillman" seems to confirm such suspicions. From the start, its promoters in the Crook County Investment Company tended to over-sell the virtues of their site and its future. This was particularly true of company president F. F. Cooper, who was described in the *Central Oregon Journal* as "running over with enthusiasm about the project, and [insisting] that they expect to have a town of 2000 population within a year and a half," with land being offered for upwards of two thousand dollars an acre, and, Cooper claimed, a thousand lots sold in the town's first ten days.

Such grandiose claims, repeated in newspapers all over Oregon, were brought to the attention of State Attorney General Crawford, whose office had only recently settled a rash of land-fraud cases involving spurious timberland claims in the upper Deschutes country. The tactics of Hillman's promoters must have aroused Crawford's suspicions instantly. Announcing an investigation, he was quoted as saying that the townsite "was apparently platted on a rockpile in a desert." As bad luck would have it, a Deschutes Valley land-agent unconnected with the project but coincidentally named Hillman was in serious legal trouble around this time; and the once catchy name of the town was further tarnished when James J. Hill was reported to have angrily denied that Cooper and Co. had ever asked his or Harriman's permission to name Hillman after them. Ultimately, under fire from all sides, accused in the newspapers of "unfair, grossly fradulent, untrue, and misleading advertising," Cooper and his cohorts were sent packing, and in November 1911, a delegation appeared before the Crook County Court with a petition to change the now-unsavory name of the town to the much more poetic "Terrebonne." Terrebone it still is.

And what of Opal City? I admit I grew up assuming that it, too, was the remnant of a railroad-era scheme in which eager and gullible locals were bilked by a team of Portland sharpies; but in truth, after reviewing both oral history and the available records, I can find no evidence to support such suspicions. Joseph Houston was well known and well respected in the region before the railroad fever hit central Oregon; his earlier Odin Falls power and irrigation project (mentioned in the article on Opal City) was not the kind of enterprise that the land-schemers and swindlers of that time and place would have pushed. The Prineville *Central Oregon Journal*, with no particular axe to grind, hailed him as "the father of Opal City," and reported with reference to his plans for the new town that he "has been in this country for more than the past year [1909, clearly in contradistinction to the hordes of outland promoters just then arriving] and has always fulfilled all his obligations to the letter. ..."

The fact is that nobody knows whether Houston, William Morfitt, Clarence Gilbert, Wilfred Jones, and the other Portland-based stockholders in the Opal City Land Company had hidden financial motives in promoting their townsite, beyond what they announced to county officials and the public: to sell residential and commercial lots to folks who wanted to be in on the founding of a new town on the railroad. Hindsight does indicate, as we will see in more detail later, that the whole venture was probably doomed to fail from the outset, and the judgment of all parties was questionable, perhaps obscured or tinted rosy-colored by the smoke of opportunity then in the air.

But it's also a fact that Walt Mendenhall did receive four thousand dollars from the land company for his homestead, a princely figure for those days. (He promptly bought his parents' homestead just north of the site, and settled there.) And it's also a matter of record that Houston and his partners did lay out some money, apparently in good faith, to foster the development of the town they were promoting; late in 1909, they retained a local well-driller, Frank Loveland, to drill a municipal well, and they also hired the Crook County surveyor, Fred Rice, to make a preliminary survey of the promised electric branch line from Opal City to Prineville.

The only evidence I've found of shady dealings in the Opal City Land Company points to an instance of we now call a "corporate takeover" from inside, but not an attempt to defraud investors and the public. On February 26, 1913, Judge Bradshaw of Crook County issued a judgment in favor of William Morfitt, Plaintiff, against Joseph Houston and his wife, stripping them of all claims to the land company and its assets, and ordering them to pay Morfitt costs and damages to the amount of $2280.76.

The case records are murky, but apparently Morfitt claimed that Houston took on undisclosed debts and mortgages in setting up the corporation and buying the townsite. Whatever the legal pretext, Morfitt's real intent, clearly, was to drive out the Houstons and take control of the company and its assets. (An earlier townsite-corporation struggle in Bend in April 1911 had led to the ouster from the Bend Townsite Company of its prominent founder, Col. A. M. Drake.) In the case of Opal City, on Judge Bradshaw's order, the property constituting the townsite was foreclosed, and then, in July 1913, put up for public auction in Prineville. Not surprisingly, William Morfitt was the only bidder, and purchased the land for twenty-three hundred dollars, only twenty dollars more than the judge had ordered the Houstons to pay Morfitt for "damages," and considerably less than the corporation had originally paid Walt Mendenhall for his homestead.

So Joe Houston, once hailed as "the father of Opal City," was summarily separated from his offspring, and suffered the insult of paying substantial damages to his corporate adversaries, as well as the injury of losing his company and his investments. The impression here of an ugly internal plot, and maybe of a crooked trial and a judge on the take, is pretty strong, but given the evidence now available, it's impossible to know for sure. No doubt this whole unsavory episode did contribute to the decline of Opal City's prospects; but we should return now to that brief period just before and just after the arrival of the railroad, when those prospects seemed bright, and (presumably) the stockholders were pulling together under Joe Houston to sell their new townsite lot by lot.

What were you buying, in 1909, if you ventured to buy a lot from the Opal City Land Company? One of our family's relics of the enterprise is a copy of the actual abstract of title conveying title from "Uncle Walt" Mendenhall to Joseph Houston and his partners; and included in the bundle is a wonderfully detailed photostat of the plat-map of "Opal City, Crook Co., Oregon," prepared by the Crook County Abstract Co., and signed by the Crook County judge and commissioners, March 1, 1911.

The shape of the town on this map is an L, tipped forward, exactly following the outline of Uncle Walt's homestead. The map has a legend indicating that its original was drawn to a scale of 1 inch = 150 feet, but this does not correspond to actual dimensions given on the map: clearly our title-copy has been reduced from an original twice as large, and in fact the original full-sized plat is on file in the Crook County Court archives. The uniform width of the legs of the L is about 1,320 feet, and the length of the long side of the property is 3,945 feet, giving an area of nearly seven million square feet. A small town, then, but many have started smaller.

On the map of Opal City, the nine streets run north and south, from First Street on the western boundary to Ninth on the east. The ten avenues run east and west, beginning with North Avenue along the north city limits, and proceeding south through Emerald, Opal, Ruby, Garnet, Pearl, Topaz, Cameo, to South (at the southern limits). The avenues are all boulevard-sized, eighty feet wide; the streets are all sixty feet, except for Second and Third, which are eighty, perhaps to set them off as primary thoroughfares.

(When the celebrated DeMoss family, Oregon's "Lyric Bards," platted their town of "DeMoss Springs" in Sherman County in the 1880s, their fancy for naming ran along artistic lines: east-west streets were to be named for famous musicians, those running north and south for great poets. How much more inspiring than the prosaic alphabetical and numerical "naming" of the streets of most Western towns, the ones that came to be.)

Within Opal City's grid of avenues and streets, a total of forty-four city blocks are marked off and numbered, all but four of them sized at 375 feet by 215, and those four (along the eastern edge of the "foot" of the L) are "half-blocks," at 225 by 215. All of the blocks are divided horizontally by fifteen-foot alleys running west and east, and serving as the backyard boundaries of each individual lot. Most blocks are divided into sixteen lots, each one hundred feet deep and fifty feet wide; some, however, are divided into smaller lots, one hundred feet deep but only twenty-five feet wide. In comparative terms, the larger Opal City lots approximate the size of typical residential lots in older American cities today, like Rochester, New York, where I lived for many years. The smaller lots, however, would be substandard today. One wonders how sixteen houses could have been crammed into one side of such a block.

The presence of the railroad in the Opal City scheme is marked by a wide right of way labeled "Central Oregon Railroad," which angles northwest by southeast across the foot of the L from First and Garnet to Third and Cameo. And true to the original announcement of the townsite, the "Opal City-Prineville Electric Line" is shown as a bold dotted line, running north from Pearl down the middle of Second, and then making a right-hand turn onto Opal and so out of town and on its way to Haystack, Lamonta, and points east.

No parks or other public spaces are marked on the plat. Perhaps, given the magnificent scenery surrounding the site, Houston and his associates didn't feel that parks were necessary; more likely, they were not willing to set aside marketable property for such civic purposes, at least not just yet, unlike their rivals in Culver, whose original plat included parks and even a college campus. On the full-scale original town plat of Opal City, the sixty-three town blocks are surrounded by twenty-five numbered but blank partial blocks. These perimeter blocks are omitted in the small town-plats that were included in each lot-title packet; and they explain how and why, in the latter, the salable town-blocks begin with number twelve and skip a couple of numbers every ten blocks. Perhaps these blank blocks around the town proper were set aside as land for parks and other civic purposes—or perhaps they were just meant to provide a buffer against encroachment on the town from farming and wildlife ... .

Studying the plat closely, one is struck by how carefully its details are worked out; this was no whimsical doodle of an imaginary town! But when one duly considers the realities of the setting and the circumstances at hand, it does seem not just visionary but a little far-fetched. The number of lots enumerated and thus for sale adds up to a grand total of nine hundred and forty. Allowing for forty or fifty of these to be designated commercial, and assuming a very low estimate of occupants per house, say three, the Opal City of the 1911 plat could have accomodated twenty-five hundred residents, or more. This is, we would say now, the stuff of promoters' dreams, not necessarily dishonest, just wild-eyed. But would we really want our local founding fathers and mothers to have been squint-eyed, hard-nosed realists, content to name their streets by numbers and letters?

The first official train—on the Oregon Trunk line—reached Madras, twenty-odd miles to the north, on February 15, 1911. For the rest of his life, my father cherished his small-boy memories of the grand celebration on that cold bright day, with its speeches, band-music, and giant outdoor banquet of roast beef. Somewhere in the family treasury there is a tattered little white silk ribbon, with "Railroad Day, Madras, Oregon, Feb. 15, 1911" printed on it, his ticket of admission and souvenir of the greatest day.

Madras was, after all, the first "real" central Oregon town the railroad builders had come to since starting their hundred-mile race up the canyon of the Deschutes, and clearly a celebration was in order; an even bigger shindig occurred when the rails reached Bend on October 5, 1911, with

James J. Hill himself in attendance, despite his advanced age (seventy-three). The Hill-Harriman race up the Deschutes had been casually terminated "back East" some time before this: the two lines remained separate beyond Madras, coming together in one single line at Metolius, where an important "division point" would be located. From here, it was easy and rapid track laying across flat terrain and deep soil, through newly moved Culver and on around Juniper Butte, reaching Opal City (the only *soi-disant* "city" on the route) sometime in spring 1911. By this time, advance work had already begun on the biggest single project on the whole route, the building of the bridge over Crooked River a mile or so to the south; and with the arrival of tracks and work-trains came great carloads of cement, huge steel beams, girders, and fittings, and battalions of men (many of them Italian and Greek immigrants) to do the job.

Opal City was ready for them, it appears, not with brass bands and speeches, but with cleared ground for the overnight creation of a tent town around a siding alongside the main track, and with commercial services already at hand. A local family named Wilson pitched a huge tent over a platform, installed an oversized range acquired from another railroad camp, and opened an eatery. My grandfather, Joe Mendenhall, and a neighbor, Art Reynolds, had already paid one hundred twenty-five dollars for a prime lot just south of the tracks (on Topaz Avenue between First and Second), and erected a livery barn and feed store there. Another neighbor, Merrill Van Tassel, an entrepreneur like his brother Ora, the founder of Vanora, paid two hundred dollars for a lot at Third and Topaz, just north of the tracks, and built a large two-story building, opening a general store on the first floor and later offering the upstairs as a ballroom for dances and socials. By April 1911, Mr. George Jones of Jones Warehouses in Bend had constructed a freight platform four hundred feet long and sixty feet wide, and this useful addition soon became the terminus of a freighting operation, hauling freight between Opal City, now the railhead of central Oregon, and the desert town of Burns, over two hundred miles to the southeast. The Oregon Trunk itself built a "Y," whereby the locomotives could be reversed and sent back north the way they had come, after more loads of girders and trusses for the bridge.

As for the eccentric homesteader mentioned earlier who hoped to get a laundry monopoly going, he was soon taking in big orders, and increasingly annoying his neighbors by constantly borrowing their water wagons to haul wash and rinse water. Apparently his plan to windlass water up from Crooked River didn't work out, or couldn't keep up with demand.

According to oral tradition, other commercial ventures operated in Opal City during the two years of its bridge-building boom. Most of these came in with the work-trains, having followed them, probably, from the start—saloons, card parlors, whorehouses, and so on, all domiciled in dirty white tents connected by trails that, by turns muddy and dusty, must have mocked Joe Houston's vision of Opal City's avenues of gems.

The labor force working on the bridge were by all accounts a rough lot, who apparently relaxed after their twelve-hour work stints by drinking, whoring, and brawling. Consequently, as its tent-city phase drew on, Opal City began to acquire a rather unsavory reputation. The rowdiness and violence persuaded the Wilsons to sell their eatery to two young men, after a few profitable but increasingly unruly months; and central Oregon newspapers seemed more inclined to cover fights and skirmishes at the camp than actual work on the "High Bridge," as it was called. In June 1911, one Thomas Miller (whose brother operated a saloon at the camp) was caught stealing a ham from a railroad car, and was subsequently shot and killed by Deputy Sheriff Thomas Williams while trying to escape being taken to Prineville for trial. In September, it was reported that an immigrant laborer, Joe Rossi, had been knifed and seriously wounded by a coworker, Joseph Nelli (the Bend *Bulletin* trumpeted "Dago Nearly Kills Man at Opal City"). And in early November there was coverage of a full-scale donneybrook involving two "automobile men" (?) and a gang of bridge workers.

But surely these were only the transient annoyances that Progress requires, and progress *was* being made, and enjoyed, in Opal City. The railroad completed the drilling of a sixteen hundred-foot deep well (perhaps finishing the job started earlier by the land company), and it announced that it would freely share the gift of water with the locals. Work-trains and passenger-carrying "combinations" were arriving and departing daily; according to a spring 1911 Oregon Trunk timetable, the train left Opal City at 8 A.M., arriving at Madras at 9:20, with service on to Portland, arriving there at 7:45 P.M. Thus merchandise, produce, and mail could be regularly sent out and received at the little depot that had been built near Van Tassel's store. One hard-pressed homesteading family nearby was especially grateful for such service: the wife's father, anxious (with good reason) about the utter improvidence of his son-in-law as a homesteader, sent up weekly shipments from Portland of food, clothing, even mops and brooms!

And the *Deschutes Valley Tribune* of Culver printed an item on July 13, 1911 that says all that needs to be said here about the impact of the railroad's coming on people's lives and how they viewed the world from Opal City. It's from a column headed "Opal City News": "Joe Mendenhall and family were passengers on Monday morning's train, bound for Sheridan, Oregon, where they will spend a couple of weeks visiting relatives." How Grandpa could leave the farm and his livery barn and feed store just before wheat-harvest is a mystery: maybe there was no crop that year. But however the trip came to pass, it's much more profitable to try to imagine Joe, Ella, and their three small children trudging early in the morning with their luggage over to the depot, climbing on a railroad car of some sort (not a Pullman), and careening behind a smoking, hissing Oregon Trunk locomotive all the way down the Deschutes canyon, and then all the way down the Columbia to Portland, where they would transfer to one of the southbound electric inter-urban local trains to Sheridan.

What a great adventure! My mother was too young then to be able to recall much of the sights and sounds of the trip, but in one of her photo albums there's a wonderful postcard-format family portrait, taken at Cal Calvert's studio (near City—now Washington—Park), while the Mendenhalls were in Portland, coming or going. They're all seated in a fanciful photo-studio mockup of an *aeroplane*, with a detailed 3-D panorama of Portland and Mt. Hood beneath them. The wings of the flying machine have been unfolded; the propellor is really spinning in front of them (you can see the blurred shaft and pulleys turning it); Joe is seriously gripping the steering wheel with both hands, with Ella, Charlcia, my mother Wilma, and Max behind her. Ella is smiling a little, and, in the spirit of the moment, is holding on to her fancy Edwardian hat. Likewise, my mother, age five, clutches hers. On the plane's whimsical tail it says "Seeing Portland." Having actually taken the train from Opal City to the metropolis, now they are after a fashion *flying*, the new century seeming to open bravely before them.

(One wonders, however, how conversations ran in the Mendenhall household a few weeks after their return to Yamhill Flat, when a southbound Oregon Trunk train going fifty miles an hour on a stretch limited to ten hurtled off the track north of Sherar's Bridge, and six people died of steam burns, including the engineer. This, too, was an image of technology at work in the new century.)

Back home, work on the High Bridge continued through fall and winter 1911-12. Some deadlines were missed, because of accidents with winches and girders (a foreman named Adams nearly fell into the gorge when some steel beams shifted, before he caught a rope and saved himself), but with the inevitability of good engineering, the two giant half-spans reached across and steadily approached each other from the opposite walls of the gorge, and at last met dead-center. Photos were taken of daring workers walking across the first linking plank or girder, and then photos of the first locomotive to cross, in late spring. On May 23, 1912, the *Deschutes Valley Tribune* reported that the bridge was completed, and added that "the Bridge Camp was moved last week from the Crooked River to the Deschutes"—where exactly, is unclear, but somewhere further south, on the route to Bend.

Quite suddenly, all the tents of iniquity, the rowdy laborers, the piles of bridge parts and gear, were gone on down the tracks. Now, having played its crucial part in the construction of the bridge, Opal City could dust itself off and get on with the business of becoming a real town, like Madras and Culver up the line, and Redmond and Bend on down it.

So everyone still on hand—the shareholders of the land company, the Mendenhalls, the Van Tassels, the Ralstons, and their neighbors—must have hoped as spring turned to summer in 1912. But it was not to be; the townsite languished without real growth or development through the decade of World War One, a party to which the expected guests did not come; and eventually, with the onset of the Great Depression, the quarter section of what had been Walt Mendenhall's homestead was sold "for back taxes" to a Yamhill Flat neighbor, Johnny Henderson, who plowed it up and planted it to wheat. No streets had been paved, very few lots had been sold (only twenty-two that I have record of); no electric lights or electric railroad lines had been installed (Joe Houston's Odin Falls power project had evidently failed, for reasons unknown); and, worst disappointment of all, so far as is known, nobody had ventured to build a residence on even one of Opal City's nine hundred forty lots. Can it even be called a ghost town, having left no abandoned, haunted dwellings, to show for its brief civic moment?

Whether William Morfitt and his fellow takeover shareholders in the Opal City Land Company simply absorbed the loss of their investments and went on their way, together or separately, is unknown. Bankruptcy seems unlikely, for the simple reason that they sold so few lots: little ventured, little gained. As for poor Joe Houston, I wonder if in later years he ever came up from Portland on the train, or drove up on U.S. 97, the new "Dalles-California Highway," and paused to survey the magnificent but unpopulated setting of his dream of a town on Yamhill Flat.

Why did Opal City fail to happen, after what seemed like an auspicious start? Paradoxically, for a venture that was consciously timed to capitalize on the coming of the railroad, it looks like the root cause of the failure was bad timing. So far as the town was meant to grow with the Oregon Trunk and the Central Oregon Railroad, it was, sad to say, preempted and outflanked on both sides by other nearby towns. On the south, it was outbid by Redmond, already a thriving farming center by the time the High Bridge was finished and the rails went on through; and on the north, by Culver, which as we have seen managed to get itself moved and ready to wheel and deal before the trains reached Opal City, and especially by Metolius, where the Hill and Harriman lines merged in 1911, giving *it* the perks of a "division point." This meant switching yards, storage and repair facilities, resident employees, and even a roundhouse—all of which Opal City might have gotten for itself, with extra time, and better luck. Metolius—whose own years of decline would come later, during the Depression—was able to apply for and get its own post office in 1910; Opal City's wasn't established until 1914. A headline in the March 28, 1911 *Central Oregon Journal* proclaimed, with gloomy implications for its rival to the south, that "Metolius Is Ready for Business."

Another paradox. Clearly the Opal City Land Company and, as we've seen, some of the home folks, foresaw that the tent-city to be sited at Opal City during construction of the High Bridge was going to be a splendid opportunity which, although temporary, would diversify the local economy, and serve to kickstart the new little town. But something very different seems to have happened by the time those acres of tents and their itinerant occupants moved on. Far from attracting permanent residents, that is, buyers of lots and builders of houses and stores, the disreputable presence of the camp seems to have turned them away. And on a strictly commercial basis, it may well be that Opal City would have developed a more stable, more sustainable economy if it had been left to itself for a few years after 1911, without the artificial and short-term incentives of the tent-town era. It's as if the elegant civic symbolism of the official townsite plat was simply trampled underfoot in the building of the bridge that was supposed to secure Opal City's growth.

Of course there were serious environmental weaknesses in the plan, as well. Chief of these was lack of water: how could a town, even a small one, thrive without a source of water for domestic and municipal needs? When the Odin Falls power project failed, the land company lost its best means of pumping water up to Opal City (which Culver succeeded in doing for itself a few years later, using a hydraulic ram). The railroad's deep well, opened for public use in December 1914, certainly simplified people's lives, but it would not have been sufficient to meet the needs of a growing town, by itself. And after a few years of domestic as well as railroad use, a shocking discovery was made about the well. Children born to mothers who drank well-water during their pregnancies developed teeth disfigured with permanently stained or mottled enamel, the result, it was later discovered, of an excess of fluoride in the water.

For farming, the Yamhill Flat country was as good as any thereabouts for dryland crops, but with an average rainfall of twelve inches or less per year, and relatively short growing seasons, only irrigation could have supported the kind of intensive and diversified farming that might have given Opal City its chance at a future. Ironically, when the long-dreamed-of North Unit Irrigation project was finally built through the Flat at the end of World War Two, its main canal was routed right around the north limits of Joe Houston's town, and parts of the townsite are now lush irrigated fields of mint, blue grass, and alfalfa.

With all this on the analytical, "what-might-have-been" side of the ledger, it's only fair, historically, to recognize that after the hurly-burly of the railroad boom had subsided, and with it the dream of a town, the home-folks remaining around Opal City (as the community was now called, in local usage and on maps) went on with their lives, apparently without undue disappointment or distress. They were mostly farmers, after all, more exactly *homesteaders*, and their first and ongoing concerns were with the stubborn land and what might be done to grow paying crops on it. Safe to say, the meadowlarks went on singing as cheerfully in the junipers as they had in 1909, when such amazing things seemed possible.

Over the next two decades, the same slow attrition of original homesteaders proceeded here as it did elsewhere in central Oregon. A long dry cycle in the climate was beginning, for one thing, and eighty or one hundred sixty acres was found to be insufficient land to allow for the necessary practice of summer-fallowing fields. So many families left Yamhill Flat for (hopefully) greener prospects, and the remaining farmers absorbed their acres (if not their dreams). Joe Mendenhall was one of the stayers. He and his brother-in-law John Helfrich continued their livery barn and feed store at the townsite for a few years, operating the only seed-cleaning service in the area; but eventually they closed down, and Joe went on with his wheat-farming and his trapping.

One homesteader who stayed but did not carry on with farming was Walt Mendenhall. He, at least, had made a good profit from the railroad adventure, on the sale of his homestead to the land company, and when Merrill Van Tassel decided to give up his store and post office, Walt bought the building and took over both functions. He served until 1940 as postmaster of what was surely one of the lowest-volume post offices in Oregon; it was understood through the branches of our family, now scattered through central Oregon, that, when possible, letters and parcels were to be brought to Opal City to be mailed, because Uncle Walt received a fee for each cancellation. Whatever its stock and sales had been in the boom days, the general store was now nicely adjusted in supply to the local demand—mostly canned goods, flour, sugar, salt, crackers, cookies, candy, soda pop. For major groceries, you went "around the Butte" to Culver.

Uncle Walt lived in the back of the store, with a wing-crippled eagle named "Old Abe" for company, and in the summertime, various grandchildren. His closest neighbors, a Japanese family named Akiyami with numerous children, lived in the depot; Mr. Akiyami served as "section-boss" for the railroad until he and his entire family were summarily rounded up after Pearl Harbor as "dangerous aliens" and sent to a federal detention camp in Tulelake, California, never to return to Opal City. But before all that, through the 1920s, upstairs in the "ballroom" of the store, community socials and dances continued, with music provided by Walt, Joe, and Bill Barber. When the Union Pacific tracks were finally extended south from Bend and into California in the late 1920s, rail traffic increased considerably, and Walt was there to greet crews when they happened to stop at Opal City—greeter, mayor, and town father all in one.

On the farm just to the north, Joe and Ella Mendenhall raised their four children, and saw them through their schooling at Opal City School, built on land donated by Walt; later, in the 1920s, my mother would teach there. After Ella died, tragically young, in 1924, Joe's mother, Nancy, now in her eighties, would come over from the Willamette Valley each summer to keep house and cook during harvest. Joe and Ella's oldest child, Max, lived at home through most of the thirties, farming with his dad and working on the railroad. When Uncle Walt took sick or went on a trip, Max stood in for him as assistant postmaster.

One of my grandfather's abiding connections with the land he had chosen for himself in 1900 was mineralogy, or to use his own word, "prospecting." After Ella died and their daughters grew up and left home for jobs and marriage, he roamed the country, especially the mineral-rich Grey Butte Hills to the east, in search of specimens—agates, fossils, traces of gold, silver, cinnabar, and so on. Often in the company of another old timer, Art Reynolds, or his son-in-law Cecil Moore, or in later years one or more of his grandkids, he "toured around" (in the family phrase for it), loading his old Plymouth down with treasure rocks of every mineral variety, and then unloading them in his front yard. As a small boy who often stayed overnight with him, I remember the inexhaustible fascination of these rock piles, and my grandfather's patient accountings of them. In the early 1950s, during the Cold War uranium-prospecting boom in the West, he and I dreamed of making central Oregon's first big uranium strike—if only we could afford to buy ourselves a Geiger counter.

The year Uncle Walt finally closed down the store and the post office, 1940, a team of New Deal-subsidized writers preparing the WPA *Oregon Guide* stopped by Grandpa's house on their way through central Oregon, and visited with him. They must have enjoyed the visit; I wish I'd been there. Here's what was subsequently published in the *Guide*—Opal City's first and only notice to travelers and to history:

> ... Right on this road [US 97] to OPAL CITY, 1 mi.,
> named for OPAL SPRINGS (reached by a steep foot trail)
> in the Crooked River Canyon 800 ft. below the canyon's
> rim. Few of the stones brought to the surface show "fire"
> but they make interesting specimens. ... At Opal City is
> the J. R. MENDENHALL RANCH (visitors welcome), in
> whose house and yard is a collection of geological
> specimens, including some rare fossil flowers, leaves, and
> animal remains gathered in the vicinity. ...

Six

QUINCEY'S LADDERS:
A FISHING TALE

※

I WANT TO TELL YOU ABOUT AN UNKNOWN STRETCH of pretty good Western trout-fishing water—but before I go any further I had better explain that I'm not going to specify latitude or longitude, or draw the route out with red dots. Anybody who really expects *that* would be capable of pestering the late Richard Brautigan for details about where to buy sections of that modular fly-fishing stream he describes in *Trout Fishing in America*. True angler-readers, the kind for whom the best verbal fish are angled for and caught, or lost, know from reading their Herman Melville that sacred bodies of water won't be found on the map; true places never are.

The true (and real) stretch of river I want to tell you everything important about, except location, has been "held," so to speak, by the men-folk in my family since the turn of the last century. Our "hold" is not based on title, deed, or riparian rights, but rather it rests on an intensely furtive and selfish occupation over many years—Trespass as Right of Eminent Domain, if you will. I'm not sure, but I believe that the land on "our" side of the river belongs to whoever owns the other side, a starveout property I will call Rimrock Farms. What this mostly absentee landlord doesn't know won't hurt him, in the view of our family council; and in our strict stewardship of the river itself, we have stopped at nothing to keep out intruders, both the idle fishing kind (it wouldn't take long to destroy these waters with rapacious angling) and the khaki-shirted kind carrying clipboards, whose appearance on rivers all over the West has signalled the advent of dams, hydro projects, destination resorts, and other official ways of killing living waters.

I have argued before the family council, however, that there is a class of good-hearted, sensitive, nonexploitive readers who might safely be shown our secret preserve, *in words*, and thus share vicariously in its rare and fragile delights, without immediately trampling all over the Western landscape in search of a new river to despoil. Perhaps many of them, I conjectured, cherish secret waters of their own, on the brain as it were,

100

and so would understand. The council was touched by this idea, and agreed to it in principle, instructing me to show such readers everything—the Ladders, the best holes and riffles, the Hotel itself—but keep them in blindfolds going and coming.

Actually, the fishing at Quincey's Ladders isn't all that magnificent, anyway; it's more dependable than anything else. But if you're with me still, despite all this secrecy, let me try to tell you a fishing story in which fishing is only a pretext. Properly told, it will be a story about how a succession of human lives has taken on shape and color and continuity from contact with the complex life of a river. Quincey's is our *haunt*, you might say: we have haunted its cliffs and pools for four generations, and in turn it haunts our lives like a tribal myth. What Major de Spain's hunting camp is to the major, the boy Ike, Sam Fathers, Boon, and the others in Faulkner's *The Bear*, Quincey's Ladders have become to my family—holy ground, the point around which all the compasses whirl.

When, after long absence, we find ourselves back in such a place, with all its remembered signs and wonders intact to our view, and still we yearn deeply, what is it we are yearning for? I'm not sure, but I'll try to tell you what I can about Quincey's Ladders, and the days and nights to which they lead.

❖

FIRST, A LITTLE NATURAL HISTORY. The river runs westwardly through a dry, sparse country, at the bottom of a four-hundred-foot deep canyon that looks to be so obviously seismic in origin that the zigs and zags of its highest rims would appear to match exactly, if ever the Pleistocene earthquake-god were to undo his drastic work. (In fact, geologists insist that the canyon has been carved out by water erosion only, and more than once.) Most of these basalt rims are sheer, and you come upon them through the juniper-and-sagebrush scablands with a vertiginous shock. Dazzling sand and antic grasshoppers, and then, at the edge of one more stride, nothing, measured in the pit of your stomach by vertical fathoms of thin air under your feet. At the bottom, in shadow, a narrow band of treetops, and here and there, shy glimpses of the river.

Along a ten-mile stretch of the canyon, there are maybe seven or eight points of access over the northern rims, and these have been whimsically identified over the years as "trails"—Ed White's Trail, the Rattlesnake Trail, and so on. One or two were widened and rip-rapped in the 1930s by the Civilian Conservation Corps, to allow livestock to reach the river, but the advantage of water and grass was more than offset by the trouble it took to get herds of sheep and cattle in and out. Most are strictly improvisations on rimrock and gravity, "wildcat trails" in local lingo, with an occasional stretch of deer-path thrown in for variety. Somehow they will get you down, down, your thighs and hamstrings aching from the strain of trying to ride on scree without starting your own personal avalanche. At the third and lowest rim, you may well pause, crane your neck to look back uphill to the high rim, and ask yourself in the gathering heat, How will I ever get back up out of here? and questions of that tone. But already it is too late to turn back: already you have begun to hear the river's voice, and smell it, and feel its breath.

Down here is a strange little lost world: of narrowly horizontal planes framed by a world of tall verticals and diagonals; of lush riverside foliage and dappled shade just below a realm of glare and bitterbrush; of green water incredibly surging through a crack in a desert. All rivers—even, I suppose, the lower Hudson—have their special enchantments: here it is the sheer *improbability* of the river and its narrow margins, a place magically out of place. At water level, the sky is only a trace of blue in a slot; there is no profit in looking up. And the sound: of water rushing endlessly over scoured rocks, drawing the cool air with it through the willow branches; not so much a sound, really, as a subtle condition of the mind's ear, soon disregarded until you go up out of the canyon, and then its absence is deafening.

The river is, on an average, maybe sixty feet across, and full of deep holes and submerged boulders; its little ecosystem extends up on both sides no more that fifty feet or so. Great brittle-limbed willows and alders lean over the edge, rigged with vines; bullrushes, ferns, water hemlock, and saw-grass (the kind God created expressly for lining creels) fringe the margin. In late spring, the syringas burst into white blossoms, lading the air with their citrus perfume; in fall the trees and vines blaze into color with the first frost.

The river's fauna is unassertive, but inescapably "on parade" through their narrow domain in search of food—upriver, and then down, and then back again. The fish, shy in their element; deer at dawn and dusk; snakes when and where you find them; businesslike minks and muskrats; several families of otters … Glancing downstream one afternoon at a sunlit pool, I was horrified in my solitude to see half a dozen apparently human heads bobbing in the foam: it was an otter family at play.

For birds, there are blue herons, locally called shitepokes, always on solitary errands upstream and down; mallard ducks, magpies, jays, orioles, tiny canyon wrens with their sarcastic laughing song descending the scale and ending in a sassy Bronx cheer, and drab water ouzels dip-dipping incessantly at water's edge, fluttering clear under after water bugs, switching elements with wonderful aplomb. High over the rims, red-tailed hawks and turkey buzzards patrol on their thermals all day; and at dusk, down on the water, the bats come out, stunting for gnats through the branches. But I digress: this is supposed to be a fishing story.

If you're a dry-fly purist, committed to waders and the fetishes of light tackle, the fishing along Quincey's Ladders probably won't interest you much. This is classic bait-fishing water, murky, turbulent, and deep, and subject in early and mid-season to dramatic fluctuations of volume and color because of cloudbursts in the river's wide upland watershed, and (in recent years) by irrigation out-takes. In times of high muddy water, it is still possible to catch fish, but we stay away—why be pushy? There is a bridge over the gorge not too far from the Hotel, and by long family habit one never drives across it in any season without looking over to check out the water's level and color, against the possibility of an expedition. The bridge is narrow and heavily traveled, and it's a wonder, now that I think about it, that such distracted reconnaissance hasn't had dire, head-on consequences.

The fish are mostly rainbows (in local usage, "redsides"), fat, a little darker than their cousins in brighter streams in this region. On the average, they run about ten inches; the family record is a twenty-three-inch lunker my brother caught a few years ago in an epic battle at Dead Cow Springs, leaping from rock to rock for half an hour, struggling to keep the fish out of the main current, falling in twice, losing his hat, smashing a toenail ... Once in a great while a brown trout will turn up; and in late summer, fishing deep, we have had brief encounters with what must have been spawning steelhead: a wrist-snapping strike, a smoking reel, pop!—and slackness is all she wrote.

In the slow waters, there are schools of great yellow-finned placid chubs, some of them a yard long and capable of giving a thrill at first strike, until, after their kind, they decide to play doggo on the bottom. Once my Uncle Max came upon what he liked to call a "pilgrim" fishing (with a spin-casting outfit and worms) in still chub-water on the other side of the river. "How's it going?" Max yelled across. The pilgrim yelled back enthusiastically. "Real good!" and held up two huge scaly chubs for proof. "You mean you *keep* those things?" "Sure, they're real good eating!" A reflective pause, then, "Well, they *are* a little boney ..."

Even the redsides rarely show themselves in this river until they've struck the hook, and then their style is more submarine and muscular than acrobatic. It is not especially difficult fishing here, but it is highly specialized, and I have seen skilled and worldly fishermen skunked all morning because they insisted on playing the river according to some preconceived style. The tackle needs to be fairly heavy: #10 hook, 4-6 lbs. leader, one or two BB shot to take the bait down, a longish fly-pole (nine feet is about standard) to facilitate reaching out through branches to good holes, and derricking fish up over cliffsides. The bait is strictly seasonal. Big yellow-and-gray salmon-flies are the thing in May and early June, merely to be stripped off streamside branches then, proof-by-convenience that God must have had people who fish with bait in mind in the ordering of the world. In cold summers, there is sometimes an awkward lull between the end of the salmon-fly hatch, and the onset of grasshoppers, to be filled, not very happily, with wet-flies or nymphs or (horrors!) worms. (Even humble bait-fishermen have their degrees of pride and shame.)

Some day the definitive treatise on the grasshopper as bait will be written, following pioneer work by Izaak Walton and Ernest Hemingway. Suffice it to say here that they are telepathic creatures, able to jump just as you decide to swat; that trout do prefer the big blue-winged variety over the little brown and tan models; that pipe-tobacco companies did grasshoppers and anglers a great injury when they discontinued metal tobacco-tins, perfect for a morning's supply of bait in the shirt-pocket; and that one clear proof that America has evolved into two nations, East and West, is that the eastern bait fishermen I know habitually put their hoppers on the hook upside-down and backwards, ass-end first. Imagine! How uncouth!

My earliest memories of fishing center on being sent out in the weeds with fly-swatter and Prince Albert can to serve an apprenticeship of catching grasshoppers. "I think maybe we ought to go fishing tomorrow," my father would say at the end of a hard stint of farmwork—and I would already be out the back door, harrying the hoppers and counting my limit of trout.

Mostly, knowing how to fish here means knowing the good waters and how to address them; Max's friend the chub-fishing pilgrim understood neither. "Good water" roughly means either broken riffles, not too swift, or deep holes with an eddying current running through them. I love the resonant and slightly pompous names affixed to preferred sites on storied rivers like the Neversink and the Rogue—Bridgeville Water, Solitude Bar, The Vicar's Temptation, and so on. Eden is long lost, broken up by our irate Landlord, but an impulse survives in us sons and daughters of Adam to name our little pockets of paradise. Here along Quincey's, all in the family, the names of the good places are appropriately casual and private: Dead Cow Springs (for years to fish it properly you had to straddle the dwindling remains of a Jersey cow); Dad's Rock (surrounded on three sides by the deepest water on the river, and named for my father, who, in his declining years, would establish himself on it sultan-like and catch his limit of big fish; now it rarely produces); the Short-ladder Hole (where a four-rung ladder delivers you to an airy pulpit in a thirty-foot cliff over a lovely hole); the Foam Hole, a kind of giant churn where, it seems to my fancy, the same delicate glyph of foam has been riding at the eye of this mighty swirl ever since stream-water first followed earthquake and flood down here; the Hotel itself, at the end of a stretch of decent water where, between an overhanging cliff and a big alder, we maintain our camp.

Not names to conjure with, and I suppose that if I had to choose the terms of an afterlife of fishing, between such modest and unstoried waters and some bright mountain-clear stream like Oregon's McKenzie or Montana's Elkhorn, I would have to opt for the latter. But isn't it, in this mixed-bag life, a toss-up of pleasure: to stalk the fish and see it thrillingly approach the fly, or to cast into a brimming eddy and trust to the fingers to detect what wonderful things are happening invisibly there in the murky depths? Contrary to the artful demands of fly-fishing, at Quincey's one can afford to lollygag and survey the scene, as long as the fingers are on duty, ready for a bump or a nibble. "Nibble again, fish-nerves," wrote that admirable Northwest bait-fisherman and poet, Theodore Roethke. Eyeless Faith, and Eagle-eyed Cunning: maybe the best of fishing is neither the one or the other purely, but a dialogue of both.

Caught up in this survey of Quincey's delights, I need to acknowledge that, like any earthly treasure, it is guarded by certain dragons and booby traps. The dragons come in the form of large well-fed diamondback rattlesnakes, which range from the upper slopes down to the river's edge. Where would you rather encounter your snake—neatly coiled on the next tussock of riverside grass you mean to step on, or buzzing fiercely, invisibly, somewhere in the scree just above you on the trail going out? Chances are, you wouldn't have to make the choice: in the course of a day's scrambling you would be given both opportunities.

The old-timer for whom Quincey's Ladders are named was so fearful of the snakes here that he took to wearing articulated sections of six-inch stovepipe as leggings. On the trail down to Quincey's a little cairn marks the spot where once in August (when snakes are shedding their skins and likely to be blind and ornery) a big diamondback launched itself from a rock just above my father as he was laboring up the slope and, making like the mythical hoop-snake, actually cartwheeled between Dad's legs, fanging the air off-balance until it vanished into some brush. And the same thing exactly happened to me two years ago, at exactly the same place. After my heart agreed to return to its proper cavity, I added some votive rocks to Dad's cairn, like any grateful Tibetan after escaping the yeti.

As for pitfalls and booby traps, there is the sheer brutal verticality of the terrain, both on the canyon-side and down at river-level. As my grandfather once cheerfully put it to a shirt-tail relative who was wheedling shamelessly to be taken to Quincey's, "The way that country lies, you're never more than a few steps from falling over a cliff, or drowning, or heat-stroke, or all three!" There is virtually no riverside at all, in the sense of sandy banks and comfortable grassy approaches, only half-submerged rocks, fiendishly slippery in rain or under wet boots. After prolonged absence from the river, one is forced to relearn a tricky sort of hop-step-and-balance that on the dance-floor might be called the Quincey Stagger. One lurches and falls a lot in any event, and hooking a big fish in fast water while *en pointe* on an egg-shaped rock a long jump from shore is a special Quincey's challenge. You know you shouldn't have gotten yourself out here—but who could resist it?

There are even vegetable intimidations. For one, water hemlock grows profusely at water-line, looking temptingly like wild celery; but its stalks and orange roots are extravagantly poisonous, as Socrates learned. And there is poison oak, growing in glossy patches immediately above the high-water line, like as not barring the only sensible route to a nice hole or stretch of riffles. As a kid, I used to wade through the stuff with impunity; and then, one summer, returning to the river pale-skinned after a first year's absence at college … pass the Calomine lotion! As if, having left home, I had returned no longer quite a native, the ingrained poison-oak resistance leached out of my system, like any pilgrim. Oddly enough, my grandfather, who was a native if there ever was one, used to be afflicted, too; having been denied access to one of his favorite holes all one summer by the spread of the shrub, he retaliated that winter by setting the patch afire. The wind came up suddenly, and you can still see where the fire almost took the whole canyonside, sixty years ago.

My grandfather and his generation were the original homesteaders of the rocky plateaus through which the river angles its way, around 1900. By his recollection he and his neighbors and their sons wasted no time charting ways over the triple rims to the river, to fish, hunt, and trap. So began the era of Anglo occupation, in which our family is apparently the last shareholder—but the canyon is haunted by evidence of an earlier era of Indian occupation, probably for the same purposes, but also, very possibly, for safety in times of intertribal conflict. At the upstream limits of Quincey country there are pictographs or "Indian writings" on the cliffs along both sides of the river, as vivid in ocher and white pigment as they are imcomprehensible: circles and curlicues, grids and peculiar graduated designs looking very much like counting-records or tallies. Caves in this section have yielded grass mats, sandals, rope, food-gathering tools, and human bones, all evidence of prolonged regular occupation, probably ending in the mid-nineteenth century.

Down at the Hotel the sense of our Indian predecessors is even stronger, a haunting indeed. Here, under the trees and along a narrow sandy beach, there was room and shelter for several families to live very comfortably, even as we do when we stay overnight. In front of camp there is a huge dished-out rock, perfect for lounging on and tinkering—and each year after the high waters had shifted the sand around it, we used to find unfinished jasper and obsidian arrowheads and chips on every side. Clearly it was a splendid place for small work and expansive talk, then as now.

Back a few feet under the cliff-overhang, in the exposed roots of the giant alder, I have found what appeared to be caches of finished arrowpoints, four or five in a pile, no doubt originally done up in deerskin bags for safe keeping. Further back, in the thicket of vines against the cliff, my brother and I once uncovered a magnificent mortar, big as a washbasin, carved out of porous lava-rock. It had been broken into two unequal pieces, probably not by accident (imagine what the merely careless loss of such a utensil would have meant), but rather by some hostile raiding party, Paiutes raiding Wascos or vice versa, stumbling on our little camp and demolishing it, while the home-folks hid out, terrified, under the rimrock.

Jeopardy and concealment, solitary flight and the arts of holing up: these are powerful themes for daydreaming. When I first read Theodora Kroeber's great story about Ishi, the last Yahi Indian, who hid away in a canyon in northern California much like this one until 1911, I knew from years of fantasizing down here on the river that she had gotten the details and feel of Ishi's experience exactly right. If Ishi had taken his refuge down here, would he *ever* have come out? As country teenagers will, my brother and I used to discuss how easy it would be—"if it came to that"—to slip away to the Hotel, and hole up indefinitely. "They'd *never* find us down here," we exulted to each other, stretched out on the big rock. Who "they" were, was never clarified in our reveries, whether the sheriff, or the Mafia, or the Russians, or the local draft board—a vagueness that allowed us to concentrate on the delicious logistics of our retreat, rather than on the necessities of it. I surmise that this fascination with the means and mystique of holing up was one of the motives that led us, years later as grown men, to rebuild Quincey's Ladders and establish the Hotel—but I'm getting ahead of myself. I must tell you about Mr. Quincey, our founder, wearer of stove-pipe armor.

Mr. Quincey came from somewhere else just after the turn of the century, and chose to take up his homestead within a quarter mile of the rimrock. In this belated homestead district, where there were good reasons why the land was so late to be offered and claimed for free— shallow, rocky soil, little rain, no surface water, short growing season— his homestead was about the most marginal of all, a wonder even to his hardscrabble neighbors. He kept to himself, grubbed his land more or less clear of sagebrush and junipers, built a dug-out hovel to live in, and eventually "proved up" on his claim and received title to it, although whether he ever cropped any of it is to be doubted. A trivial consideration, anyway, in Mr. Quincey's unusual scheme of things. He was preparing to be an *entrepreneur*!

Around 1911, the long-promised railroad was reaching into this country from the north, and, as he had it calculated, the great enterprise would be held up for at least two years while a bridge was being built over the canyon, some miles up the north rim from Mr. Quincey's homestead. A wretched little city of wall-tents and lean-to's sprang up, as its counterparts had all over the West, consisting of the laborers, mostly Irishmen, Greeks, Italians, and Chinese, and an unofficial support-team of whores, gamblers, and publicans. What in Mr. Quincey's speculating eye would they all need, that only he could provide? *Laundry!*

If you're going to take in laundry, you need water. Mr. Quincey, out on his rim, had plenty of it in view—only it was flowing about four hundred vertical feet below him. So, nothing daunted (except for snakes), he threw together a rickety hundred-foot sequence of wooden ladders running from ledge to ledge over the lowest rim, for access to a deep and slow-moving stretch of the river; and then he built wooden towers on each of the three rims straight above this pool; and then—somehow— he contrived a cable tramway from canyon-rim to river over these towers, with a windlass at the top to make it go. Then he descended to the river with a number of five-gallon cans, filled them, hooked them to the cable, ran back up the ladders, scrambled up the rest of the canyon wall to the high rim, and then began to crank the windlass.

Against all odds, it worked—worked well enough, according to local legend, for Mr. Quincey to maintain his monopoly on the laundry needs of the railroad camp for a couple of years, at least, until the bridge was completed, and the construction crew moved on. Every pioneer family hereabouts has photos of the bridge nearing completion, its half-arches jutting out to each other from the opposite sides of the canyon, mathematically yearning to meet smack in the middle. Men stand facing each other at the ends of the spans, or fearlessly walk across on a plank thrown over the gap—how pleasant to think that they are all wearing clean union suits and britches from Mr. Quincey's steaming tubs!

His local career seems to end here: perhaps he just packed up his laundry and moved on with the railroad. But there is one final bizarre notice of Mr. Quincey, connecting him with the Outer World. In the early 1930s word reached his old central Oregon neighbors that he had been found dead in Los Angeles, apparently a victim of robbery and murder. He was identified, police said, only because they found some tax-receipts in his pocket—receipts for the county property taxes he had faithfully paid all those years after he had left his rimrock homestead and laundry. He must have meant to come back to the river someday, after all: I can understand that.

Anyway, his jury-rigged ladders opened up a fine stretch of river to my grandfather and his son and nephews and eventually, when he married into the clan, my father. On through the Depression and into the 1940s there was regular traffic on the river from our family; on the far side, the owners of Rimrock Farms mounted various engineering projects, all versions of Quincey's Folly—moving water up out of that gorge onto the plateau where it could do some good. One scheme involved a huge hydraulic ram, whose slow pumping cycle—*ka-CHUG! ka-CHUG!*—echoed up and down the canyon for years. And there was even a hydroelectric plant, to generate pumping power for our unwitting "landlord" across the river; the project didn't pan out, but his turbine assembly is still in place at the end of a crude spillway, overgrown with ferns and dripping moss, like some undiscovered Mayan idol—made in Schenectady, New York.

Meanwhile, as world and local history was being made, the river rose and fell, muddied and cleared in its seasons, and on "our" side, anglers came down, angled, and went home, and brooded on their luck. Came a sad day: Grandpa, coming out Quincey's Ladders, decided that they were no longer safe (were they ever?) and reported to us that he had thrown the top section over the cliff to end their use. And I'd never even been on them yet! Came another sad day: Grandpa, who into his seventies was still fishing the river solo, announced, after coming out very late one evening and scaring us all, that he wouldn't be going down again. It was like a banishment; how to imagine the river without him?

But my brother and I were growing up, and the river was waiting for us in our turn. How we happened to restore Quincey's Ladders and initiate the heyday of the Hotel is a pleasant illustration of the Law of the Fruitful Screw-up. We had laid plans to climb Mt. Hood one Sunday, but when we arrived at Timberline Lodge at daybreak, I found that I had brought myself a pair of left-footed climbing boots. Trying to salvage some part of the day thus botched, my brother proposed that we turn back, sort out my proper footwear, and check out the river for the first time this year; specifically, see if we could test our rock-climbing skills against what remained of Quincey's Ladders. So that's what we did—and in the course of that rescued day it dawned on us both that if we could restore the Ladders, we could also build a real fishing camp downriver at the Indian site under the overhanging cliff.

Uncle Max joined the project enthusiastically, and that fall, while I was away at college, he and Jim worked at it with a single-mindedness approaching Mr. Quincey's, but with higher standards: they relied less on baling-wire and more on sturdy juniper spars and new nails, and even drove in rock-climbing pitons and bolts for extra security. Max added an ingenious derrick for hoisting heavy packs up and down so they needn't be carried on the Ladders; and he went on to build, almost single-handedly, the deck under the big alder. It was left to him, fittingly, to christen it "the Hotel"; he was from the start its genial proprietor and host.

Those were the good times, all right. Two or three times a summer, generally on a signal from Max that "the river looks pretty clear," we would descend, and encamp—Max, a bachelor of leisure and independence, would go down early, blithely carrying his little dog Mousie down the Ladders with his belt cinched around its middle as a handle; then Dad and I, our summer antagonisms put aside, would arrive at mid-morning; then Jim would hurry down after work, in time for supper and evening fishing. For Dad and Max, in their late fifties, the Hotel's accomodations meant that they could divide the trip down and the trip out by at least a night's rest on the river: the one-day sprints in and out were getting to be too much for them. Max often stayed four or five days and nights after the rest of us came out. "You don't really get into the rhythm of it until about the third night," he'd say, and he was right. I fantasized Max as Ishi; certainly they were much alike in age and appearance, in possession of solitude, in geniality and patience. They would have understood each other. I also sometimes wondered, thinking of the over-determined academic life I was preparing to enter "on top," whether after a full week down here I would be good for anything in the workaday world.

Another of Max's sayings, which our hillbilly forebears probably brought with them from Tennessee, was "Always eat the best food first." And how we ate, first and last! If corn on the cob and fried potatoes attending on pan-fried trout unlimited doesn't sound like a Roman banquet, take it on faith: in this setting, in this company, it was. At night, Jim and I usually swam a bit in the pool in front of camp, the dark water very cold on our loins and full of reflected stars; and then, the four of us side by side in our bags on the planks of the Hotel deck, the endless susurrus of the river in our ears, we slept.

They were nights and days of the kind that in memory seem to make up in heights and depths what they inevitably lacked in extension. A few more such summers, and then my father's always uncertain health broke—a heart attack, a terrible spinal injury, another heart attack, and a major operation on his spine. I was living in upstate New York by then, and coming back to the ranch for a month or so each summer. I'd make an obligatory run to the river, sometimes with Max or Jim, sometimes solo, but it was like a ritual no longer fully believed in, and Dad's wistful interest in the state of things at the Hotel was hard to take. Though nothing was said, we all knew he'd never go down again.

But he did—incredibly enough, the next summer after his operation. It was one of those weird knots of circumstance that give density and color to the grain of a family's history. My brother's son Bill was twelve that summer, just about the age at which his father and I had, in our turns, been offered to the river for the first time—and how could we take Bill down, and not his grandfather, if there was any possibility of his going? Clearly he was making another of his fierce recoveries, and finally we asked the question-of-no-return: did he feel up to going? He reckoned maybe so. One wishful/willful assumption led to another; the urge to somehow spite necessity by celebrating the boy's first trip to the river and the old man's miraculous return to it was too strong for anybody's good sense to resist, even my mother's.

So there we were one August morning, Bill and his grandfather and me, standing at the head of the Ladders at cliff-edge, looking down. The old pattern was in effect: Max was already down, making camp, Jim would come later. What had I gotten myself into? The Ladders had never looked so sheer, ill-made, and treacherous; the river far below us had never looked so glitteringly hostile. I ran through my catechism of doubts one last time. I'd never forgive myself if something happens here, I thought, and yet I'd never forgive myself if we didn't try it. If Dad was having his own misgivings, he wasn't showing them: "Well, what are we waiting for?"

So—-first Bill and then (protestingly) Dad, I roped them up and belayed them all the way down; at least there would be a semblance of some prudence here at the outset of the adventure. At last—both of them on firm ground under the cliff: by God we'd made it! I left the rope in a snarl at the foot of the Ladders and joined Dad and Bill where they stood surveying the water, one for the first time, the other, as it turned out, for the last.

I was well on my way to being choked up by the momentousness of it all, and blurted, "Well, Dad, how does it look to you?" It had been four years. He vizored his eyes with one hand and scowled. "OK, but I've seen it look better—a little high, I think. Fish will be deep." If I was disappointed by his matter-of-fact response, I shouldn't have been. Wholly in character—and here it was anyway, needing no grace notes, a dispensation of joy, given and taken as a fact. Without another word, we collected our packs and fishing-gear, and headed for the Hotel.

❖

IT IS ANOTHER DAZZLING SUMMER MORNING, twenty-odd years later. My own son has just negotiated the Ladders for the first time, showing good moves, and against my barely contained anxiety and pride at seeing him venture down the cliff over Quincey's devious route, he tells me when we reach the bottom, "It wasn't nearly as bad as I expected, Dad." He has, already, his grandfather's gift of understatement; it is a good gift.

Before us, son (I do not say out loud this morning), behold the river— how it brims and boils as always in its rocks, high and dark-green because of last week's rains; never-ending, joining the mountain springs and the broad ocean, joining past and present, joining the dead, the living, and the yet-to-be-born. Son, it is not in my power to give you the river, or its mysterious and alluring fish, or the otters that frolic in its pools, for in truth, none of us owns any part of it; in our four or five generations of coming here its great rushing voice has not paused once to hearken to the claims of our human voices. To love the river, you must study to become part of what it owns, and keeps, unawares, in a custody as light and timeless as the foam that rides these eddies. That is where all the river's old people are; it has them, safe—your grandfather, and now Max, and your great-grandfather, and Mr. Quincey the builder of ladders, and the Indians who on a bright morning like this one would come out of the trees and sing.

I say nothing of this to my son. Instead, I point downriver and tell him, "This is the way to the Hotel."

Seven

THE CANYON

⚜

WHEN YOU GROW UP WITH MOUNTAINS constantly in view, you're likely to develop a special susceptability to *canyons*, as their conceptual opposites and antitypes. As a child, looking daily from majestic Mt. Jefferson in the western distance to our little canyon in the foreground, I used to wonder if maybe mountains were created in the same cataclysmic transactions that excavated canyons—the rocks and dirt scooped out of the one, to be heaped up high in the other. In a sparse country that gives little away, it seemed like a plausible economy.

Be that as it may, although the picture postcards don't emphasize it, central Oregon's landscape is at least as much shaped by canyons, gorges, gullies, ravines, and gulches as it is by mountains and buttes. Early explorers and trailblazers could and did stay out of the Cascade Range, but the canyons of the land were unavoidable and determining barriers to travel, and the deepest of them—the Gorge of the Crooked River— stopped the empire builders cold until 1912.

There is, it seems to me, something uncanny, something "mental" about canyons, as if they were as much states of mind as brute geological structures. You walk into one as into a kind of rugged absence, a gap in the earth's dependable floor into which the air, the horizon itself, plunges right along with you. You abruptly leave the workaday surface world for another place, with its own gravity and its own slotted sky and tilted light. You go out of the dry flatlands half-expecting to find a different world at the bottom, and to the extent that there's running water there, your otherworldly expectations will be fulfilled, in lush greenery, cool air, shade. When Orpheus descended after his lost Eurydice, was it into a canyon like one of these?

It's the way of canyons, of course, to eventually run into other, bigger ones, and so on out and down to the catchall of the ocean. Mentally traveling *up* such a system, following up a tributary of a tributary of, say, the great Columbia, may seem perverse, like the deadly procedure of an inept storyteller who insists on running up every branch and side-channel of the story until the main course of it is lost from view and past caring about. But canyons out here aren't story lines (although they may be full of stories); if they ultimately give way to bigger chasms, they nonetheless have their own intense local identities. Somehow, if they're all the same, they're also all different from one another, each one with its own rough charm. It's *that* I want to catch and celebrate here if I can, focusing on the modest example I can see out my window as I write this, clear from its head here at the west edge of Agency Plains, down to its mouth on the Deschutes River.

Cars and trucks roar endlessly up and down its one human "improvement," a highway cut and grade below the northside rim. Most of this traffic, lunging over from Portland and back on weekends, goes at best dimly aware of the deep declivity beyond the guard rail in the few minutes it takes to climb or descend the grade and be on their impatient ways. And most locals also make the passage heedlessly, I imagine—except when the road turns icy. So our vehicles have taught us to transit the landscape, *en passant* and blinkered, either because we're hellbent to get from *there* to *there*, and *here* is only one brief phase of the journey, or because we've made the trip so often for so long that there seems to be nothing left to look for.

Now and then all this changes for the passersby. Cars have gone careening off the grade and into the canyon, end over end; pathetic little memorials of yellow and blue plastic flowers sometimes mark where the rocks below met them and their passengers. On a more positive note, just recently I noticed, on a point of rimrock just below the head of the grade, a wonderful ensemble of teetery rock sculptures, like the *inuksuk* stone effigies the Inuits erect as locational monuments in the Arctic. Probably just the work of someone—maybe with kids—stranded there for a few hours because of a flat tire or a blown radiator; but I want to count the perpetrators as artists, not vandals. They at least left the canyon with a story, connecting themselves to the place. I plan to tend those roadside *inuksuks* solicitously—until the frost and the winds bring them down next winter.

Part of the charm of canyons, I think, even minor ones like ours, lies in the way they seem to accumulate and preserve local information, both natural and human, and intermixed. Evidence of what has gone on along and under these rims, from eonic times to last spring, tends to abide here against the forces of change and distraction that we contend with on the surface, "under the sun," as Ecclesiastes puts it.

The bones of our celebrated cutting horse, Flicka, still lie strewn along the creek, where she died, thirty years ago; mashed washtubs and broken bottles from the original homestead household of the Gard family have washed below the rim but are still lodged in the creekbed; red-tailed hawks still nest in the Sandstone Cliffs, where my father remembered them nesting when he was a boy; just last week I noticed that the imposing badger-hole nearby was being retenanted once again. And below the columnar basalt of the cliffs, halfway down, where the highway grade cuts deeply into the hillside, lies an important site of Pliocene Era leaf fossils, dating back several million years.

Canyons are the memory of our landscape.

ON A GOOD GEOLOGICAL SURVEY MAP, this canyon runs roughly three miles east to west across Sections 9, 8, and 7, in Township 10 South, Range 13 East, descending from about 2,300 feet at its eastern head, to its confluence with the Deschutes River, at 1,400 feet. It begins with unusual abruptness in a rough pasture just east of our machine shed, with a jump-off over twenty feet of cliffs. Almost immediately it widens out to maybe a quarter mile between the north and south rims; eventually, as it melds into the canyon of the Deschutes, it fans out to nearly a mile. It has no tributary canyons on the north side, but on the south there are three, coming in every half mile or so: the Gard Canyon (named for our homesteading family; Harry Gard homesteaded our place, and was one of the fathers of the North Unit Irrigation Project); the Bob Dunn canyon (after an early farmer who lived near it); and a nameless stub of a canyon—really, more of a ravine—that comes in from the south just behind the old Campbell place. A small stream, usually called Campbell Creek, runs along the main canyon bottom, gathering volume and force from the side canyons and hillside springs fed by irrigation wastewater on Agency Plains. Before irrigation (which began in 1948) the creek was, in most years, intermittent, but now, with the water table substantially raised, it runs year-round.

Geologically, the canyon is typical of its kind in this country—carved through layers of basalt and lava by the patience of water (although it's easy to imagine that earthquakes may have helped out, too). The rimrocks are composed of grey "Agency Plains" basalt over a hundred feet thick, dating far back to an era of active lava and mud flows, said to have emanated from Round Butte, about ten miles to the southwest. So our canyon in its present configuration must be younger than that. Possibly it (and its tributaries) began to be carved out by glacier runoffs at the end of the Pleistocene Era.

As in any canyon, walking down is in effect a descent into layers of geologic time. Just above the Gard Canyon's mouth, for example, there is, on both sides, a stratum of compressed sandstone known as the Sandstone Cliffs, bearing witness to a time before the age of volcanoes and mud-and-lava flows, when much of this country was under the waters of enormous inland lakes. Half a mile further down is the fossil site I've already mentioned, whose discovery in 1935-36 (when the highway grade was being excavated) put the canyon on the paleobotanical map, so to speak. The road builders dug into a layer of whitish tuff which, when blasted into big boulders, was found to be studded with fossil leaves— not just prints, but the original organic material petrified in black, preserving the details of each leaf minutely, as if in a black and white negative.

Word of this discovery passed from highway engineers to Phil Brogan, dean of central Oregon's historians and naturalists, and from him on to Professor Luther Cressman of the University of Oregon (later celebrated for his excavations of the Fort Rock and Long Narrows paleo-Indian sites), and so on to Professor Ralph W. Chaney of the University of California. Chaney arranged to meet at the site with Brogan, Lon Hancock (one of Oregon's pioneer paleontologists), and a group of interested locals, including Lewis "Turk" Irving, a Madras entrepreneur and bon vivant. Chaney declared on the spot that it was a momentous discovery, the first Pliocene Era flora fossils ever discovered in Oregon. His scholarly excitement must have been contagious—"Turk" Irving reportedly choked on his customary quid of chewing tobacco, and had to be sluiced out with a canteen.

As a boy, I used to examine the fossils in these boulders, without knowing anything about their significance. But in 1990-91, excavations to widen the highway cut opened up new portions of the site for study, allowing a local paleobotantist, Mel Ashwill, to review Chaney's work and add to it for the scientific record. According to Ashwill, the leaves (and some casts of tree trunks) came from a grove of deciduous trees that were overwhelmed, along with everything else in this part of the Deschutes drainage, by a hot volcanic mud flow, about 5.3 million years ago. Ashwill and others have noted that exactly the same process of leaf preservation seems to be happening in the mud-flows from Mt. St. Helen's eruption in 1980—fossils-in-the-making from our own time.

In Ashwill's tally, the fossil leaves are from tree and shrub species still extant in the Northwest, though not necessarily in central Oregon. They include spirea, Oregon grape, cottonwood, black and white oaks, madrona, hawthorn, willow, and box-elder. Professor Chaney thought he had found a new variant of plum and named it in honor of Turk Irving, *Prunus irvingi*, but later, sad to say, had to rescind the discovery as an error. Given the drastic upheavals in landform and climate here over five million years, it says something about the persistence of plant life that, in the bottom of our canyon, immediately below the fossil site, willows and cottonwoods still flourish, lighting the streambed with their golden radiance every autumn, as they must have done back in Pliocene times, no less beautiful then for the lack of our kind to appreciate them.

From this fossil record, one would have to conclude that the dominant canyonside vegetation of today—scrubby junipers, sagebrush, chemise, chokecherries, Oregon balsam, wild roses—appeared on the scene later, probably in the same drying and chilling of the climate that killed off the madrona, oaks, and elders of the Pliocene record.

Ashwill notes that no animal fossils have been found in or around the site (an observation that somewhat assuages my boyhood disappointment at never finding such artifacts in our canyon), but he adds that, five million years ago, there were certainly horses, wolves, bears, buffalo, deer, antelope, and various kinds of big felines in these precincts—and also camels, rhinos, and mammoths! Today's bestiary seems considerably less heroic, but in going up and down the canyon I wouldn't trade the critters of the Pliocene for these of the present: mule deer, occasional elk, coyotes with their immemorial dens in the rimrocks, badgers, rockchucks (the local name for groundhogs), diamondback rattlesnakes, bobcats,and at least a rumor of a pair of mountain lions, and several species of imported game birds: China pheasants, chukhars, and just recently, wild turkeys. And overseeing everything, the turkey buzzards, red-tailed hawks, and great horned owls.

Maybe it's just wishful thinking on my part, with an eye on current reports of wholesale global extinctions, but I have the impression that the canyon's population of wild fauna has actually *increased* over the last thirty or forty years. We still rent portions of it out for cow-and-calf pasturage April through November, but with our own noisy and commotious family farming operations shut down since the 1960s, and my mother living alone at the head of the canyon for many years since then, it seems to be taking on the ambience of a wildlife preserve. Surrounded as we are by a busy highway and hi-tech irrigated farms, we are nonetheless visited by more wild creatures out of the canyon than I can remember from my boyhood. Last fall, my mother watched a doe unconcernedly nursing her fawn directly in front of the house; this winter, a pair of coyotes regularly hunted for mice in the windrows in the same field, and a rough-shinned hawk, wintering here from its homeland in the far north, has taken up hunting rights in the south pasture. They're all here, of course, because of the haven (and food supply) of the canyon. The coyotes and the hawks would like it here even better, no doubt, if I reintroduced chickens on the ranch, but why tamper farmer-like with a natural balance reasserting itself?

In truth, the human presence in our canyon has never been very intense or intrusive. The county assessor classifies it as "unimproved land," and although he assesses its market value at an improbable $680 an acre, its topography is such that you wouldn't want to build a house on it, and Oregon's strict land-use laws would forbid such a California-style folly, anyway. My father always said, with the canyon in mind, that it was a good thing to have some land so rough that nitwits with four-wheel-drive rigs wouldn't even be tempted to try driving them across it.

If not occupation, or vehicular passage, there must have been regular Indian travel up and down its bottom and slopes—who knows how far back, but with the establishment of the Warm Springs Reservation in 1855 it became a regular route up onto the Agency Plains and so on east to camas-digging beds and hunting grounds in the foothills of the Ochoco Mountains. Our place at the head of the canyon seems to have served as a campsite and way station for such expeditions, judging from the grinding stones, digging tools, and arrowheads we've found over the years. With the construction of the Oregon Trunk railroad up the Deschutes in 1910-11 (abandoned in the 1920s) and the advent of wagons and buggies and then autos, a steep roadway was scratched out of the north side, named the Vanora Grade for the railroad community being promoted downriver. The Vanora Grade must have been challenging to Model Ts both going down and coming up, but its carefully rip-rapped roadway is still passable, winding down above the busy three-lane traffic of Highway 26.

Over its human history, the canyon has acquired a variety of names, none of them authoritative or official even in local usage. The earliest name for it that I know of is Indian: *totwanna*, as recorded in the journal entry of Dr. William McKay for February 9, 1867. McKay was on his way from the Warm Springs Agency to resume his mission of harrying Paiute bands in eastern Oregon. Making a late start from the Agency, he crossed the Deschutes and "camped at Totwanna Creek" (*Oregon Historical Quarterly,* Summer 1978, p. 156). Presumably *totwanna* is a Wasco Chinook (*kiksht*) word. At least in the form given by Dr. McKay, its meaning is obscure, but it seems to derive from the *kiksht* root-word *-twana,* meaning "following" or "going along with"—as the creek follows the canyon, and travelers followed both.

Modern maps like the US Geological Survey "quad" map identify the creek as "Campbell Creek," in recognition of a prominent pioneer family which settled on the rich bottom land near the Deschutes before 1900. John E. "Ed" Campbell raised a big family here, held a contract for carrying the mail from The Dalles to Prineville, and built and operated the first ferry across the Deschutes in these parts. His son John L. acquired the place around 1914; he and his wife Ella were our beloved "canyon neighbors" when I was growing up. So Campbell Creek and by implication Campbell Canyon seem right in terms of commemorating the extensive contributions of the Campbells to local history.

But old-timers used to identify the canyon by another name, and to flush out *its* significance we must briefly turn aside from our main route, as if straying into an interesting side-canyon. I used to hear them call it, seemingly without racial inflection, Nigger Brown Canyon. No one seemed to remember much about Brown, except that he was indeed an African American who had homesteaded or perhaps squatted before the turn of the century in the canyon just below the Campbell Place. The racist part of his name troubled me when I was growing up, but I confess I didn't question it until my college-age children, hearing about Nigger Brown for the first time, challenged it indignantly. We agreed then and there that it *was* an outrage, a part of our central Oregon heritage that we couldn't live with. Couldn't we find out enough about Mr. Brown to reclaim him and the canyon from the casual racism of his white neighbors? Could we at least restore to him the dignity of his full name?

Some sleuthing in county and federal land records brought Mr. Brown at least a little out of the shadows. He was, in fact, John A. Brown, and he filed a homestead claim on 160 acres on both sides of Campbell Creek, on December 5, 1881, in Wasco County Courthouse in The Dalles, making him one of the earliest homesteaders in all of what is now

Jefferson County, and very likely the first African-American landowner in central Oregon. By 1888, according to the records, he was forty-eight years of age, was married to a Mexican or possibly an Indian woman named Mary, and they had had a child, as reported in the *Prineville Review* of March 10, 1888: "Born—to the wife of John A. Brown of Warm Springs, on Thursday Feb. 16, a daughter."

On April 6, 1891, his homestead claim was duly ratified by the U.S. government, and he received title to his land; by this time, according to his petition, he was living in a seventeen by thirty foot house "with one window and three doors," had twenty acres in cultivation (grain hay), and was tending an orchard of 147 fruit trees. He listed his farming equipment as "one plow and harrow, hoes, shovel, wagon, and one span of horses ..." Clearly, from this evidence alone, he was much more than just the transient squatter of the old-timers' references.

There's virtually no trace left of John Brown's house site and garden on the north side of the creek; erosion and silting from floods have either washed away or covered every sign except for an old yellow rosebush, now huge, and a few sections of iron pipe that must have run from his spring upstream into the house. His fruit trees on the south side of the creek have long since died or been cut down. In a Campbell family album, there are two photos of the house and grounds as they stood around 1900, after the Browns had left and Ed Campbell and his family were briefly living there. To the original two-story board-and-batten house, a one-story addition had been built, making an attractive T-shape. Just east of the house in the photos stands a line of flourishing Lombardy poplars, pioneer central Oregon's ubiquitous shade trees. Again, the impression of a well-planned, purposeful operation is strong: John Brown obviously knew what he was up to as a homesteader.

In her memoir of her family's homesteading experiences on Agency Plains, *Some Bright Morning,* Bess Stangland Raber recalls stories about John Brown, probably collected from John Campbell and from her father Frank. Referring throughout to "the Nigger Brown Place," she notes that he "irrigated his place, and raised vegetables, which he peddled in Prineville. There he liked to patronize saloons. After imbibing, he tended to get loud and boastful. Then he might shout, 'I've got two thousand head! I've got two thousand head!' Since this was cattle country and two thousand was an impressive number, customers viewed him with respect until he shouted, 'Yes, I've got two thousand head of cabbages!' " (p. 307).

It's pleasant to infer from this anecdote that John Brown was enterprising, sociable, and had a sense of humor. But the little we've recovered about him and his two decades on his land still seems negligible in comparison to what we don't know. Where did he come from, and how did he arrive in central Oregon when he did? And how and why did he and his family leave the homestead, around 1900?

To the first question, we might observe from his birth-date, 1840, that he was the right age to have served during the Civil War in one of the Union's Black regiments, and then conjecture that he went on, after the war, to join one of the Black Indian-fighting detachments in the West, the so-called "buffalo soldiers." If so, possibly he participated in the Bannock War campaign in eastern Oregon in 1878, and then decided to muster out and take up a farming career near Warm Springs—but who knows?

Questions about how and why Brown left his place are equally frustrating, given what we don't know. It must have been around the turn of the century; by 1904 or so, others held title to the place, and a succession of families rented the house, before Ed Campbell bought the property. Years later, John Campbell's recollection from boyhood was that the Browns had left rather abruptly, promising to come back but never doing so. By 1900, John Brown would have been sixty, well past middle age in those times. Was there some racial incident or situation that provoked him to sell out and leave, or was he simply tired of raising cabbages for the Prineville market, and resolved to make a new start elsewhere, despite his age?

A possible clue to John Brown's life after leaving the canyon is recorded in the Oregon Census for 1900. His name is not listed under the Warm Springs precinct of what was then Crook County, but the census taker in Ireland Precinct of Crook County, a stretch of unsettled country reaching from present-day Sunriver and Lapine clear to the future site of Bend, recorded one "John Brown, negro," aged sixty-four, born in Canada, married to "Mattie," a Paiute Indian. Whether our homesteader or not, this John Brown became a well-known local character, raising cattle, reportedly mining gold in the summer, and trapping in the winter. *Oregon Geographic Names* lists Brown's Creek and Brown's Mountain south of Crane Prairie, both named for a Negro homesteader who ran cattle in that country. And in Russ Baehr's *Oregon's Outback* there are tales about the possible whereabouts of John Brown's gold-mining sites and stashes of gold.

Could this be our man of the canyon, relocated despite his age in the even more remote and challenging high country in the Cascade foothills south of Bend? Perhaps "Mattie," his Paiute wife in the census, was really Mary, whether Indian or Mexican; perhaps he was careless about his age, giving it as sixty-four in 1900, when according to his homestead deposition of 1888 it would have been sixty.

The 1900 census entry for "John Brown of Ireland Precinct" offers another very peculiar detail. He is said to be by profession a trapper, but also a "servant" to one "Hiram Palmer, aged 78"! What "servant" meant then, out here on the Oregon frontier, is anybody's guess—certainly not a gentleman's gentleman; more likely a hired man/caretaker for the aged Mr. Palmer, whoever *he* was. Maybe, if the two John Browns were really one, taking on such employment had provided some initial income for him and his family while he was setting up his new household.

The current owners of the old Campbell place have given me one more, really haunting addition to what has become the John A. Brown File. One day in the summer of 1992, soon after they moved into the place, an elderly African-American man came to their door, identified himself as a grandson of John Brown, and asked if he could look around for signs of his grandfather's homesteading life. The visitor's name and address, and how, on the basis of what family information, he'd been able to find his way to the canyon, weren't recorded. Obviously he must have known quite a bit to have found the place at all, and the thought of a family tradition incorporating Mr. Brown's homesteading achievements in Central Oregon is pleasant to mull over. But, alas, it doesn't shed much light on his life. Maybe, however, we do know enough about him now to propose—beginning with local usage—that the canyon be officially named John Brown Canyon, in honor of its first homesteader, an important but forgotten central Oregon pioneer.

AT THE HEAD OF THE CANYON, right on the edge of the rimrocks in fact, there used to be a massive stone fireplace and chimney, the stones so cunningly laid together that they seemed to interlock, no mortar needed except for mud. Playing around and on it, roasting picnic hotdogs on its hearth, I assumed it would stand forever—until one spring I came home from college to discover that it had utterly collapsed into a pile of oddly assorted rocks. Maybe the patient sabotage of frost brought it down, or possibly a minor earthquake. Now even the pile of rocks has vanished under the sod.

No one recalls who built the fireplace, or when, but in the 1880s, the cabin it warmed was probably the only inhabitable dwelling on Agency Plains, and in the dreadful winter of 1884-85 it was occupied by a hard-pressed sheepherder named Whistling Smith. Smith was in charge of several thousand sheep owned by Alonzo Boyce (later judge of Jefferson County), and a sizeable part of the flock was wintering in the canyon. As the snow piled up deeper and deeper (eventually it reached a depth of four feet, and thousands of sheep died), Whistling Smith left a note in the cabin for his boss to the effect that he was going to walk down the canyon to check on the sheep and visit with John Brown. A second note reported that breaking trail that far had proved to be too much for one day, and so he was setting out again the next day. He never reached Brown's farm, and the next spring Alonzo Boyce found his body under a juniper tree about a half-mile up from his destination.

For some reason, Whistling Smith's remains (including his boots) were never decently buried, and eventually ended up in a wooden box, which I used to see, shiveringly, as a small boy, until box, bones, and boots were consumed in a wildfire that ran up the canyon. Playing below the rimrocks, I used to scare myself with fantasies about Smith's ghost, trudging up and down the trail, and, mindful of the "The Whistler" radio program with its eerie theme-music, I even tried to summon his shade by whistling—but I never hit on the right tune.

Poor Smith's death from exposure is the only known fatality in the canyon (except for several car-wrecks off the grade), but there have been some close shaves over its rugged terrain. My aunt Lela Gard Ramsey used to tell about her father Harry Gard's near-miss when walking home after a visit to the Campbells one summer day in 1903. He'd waited to leave for home until an intense rainstorm blew over, but as he came around a bend, he saw a wall of muddy water rushing down on him. In the nick of time he was just able to scramble up the south canyonside as the torrent roared on down, carrying everything with it; but then, because all of the south-side branch canyons were also at full flood, he had to walk clear around them to reach home, twelve miles of muddy slogging instead of three.

My own father's misadventures in the canyon were frequent, usually involving rattlesnakes, coyotes, fractious horses, or these in combinations. One August day, he and I were riding up the last steep slope out of the canyon below our house, when a rattler, probably shedding its skin and therefore blind and ornery, began to rattle above him, and then struck, lost its balance and rolled down the slope, coiled and struck again, rolled further, and so on, like the mythical hoop snake, right between the front legs of Dad's horse. The horse, a temperamental gelding named Blue, bucked all the way down to the creek and then all the way up to the rim. It was a great show while it lasted.

Another time, in a period when we were trapping coyotes for the bounty, Dad found one in a trap, clubbed it to death (he thought), and tied the carcass on behind the cantle of his saddle. Halfway up the canyon, the poor coyote came to life, scratching, biting, snarling, and old Blue went berserk. Somehow in the first few bucks, Dad's tight Levi jacket got caught over the saddle horn, so that he could neither turn around to handle the coyote, nor abandon ship, which would have been the sensible thing to do. So he grimly held on, like a rodeo bronc rider without a hazer to ease him off after the whistle, until the desperate coyote bit through the saddle thongs and tumbled to the ground.

Much earlier, in the 1920s, Dad survived a scrape that very nearly cut off his part of the Ramsey lineage (and thus mine). He and his older brothers had persuaded Harry Gard to let them install a motorized pump down in the canyon, where a copious spring comes in. With this installation, they were able to pump water up onto the Plains and into a big cement reservoir, from which it ran by gravity to the houses of various Ramseys ... in effect, a private domestic water system. The pump and motor were housed in a little two-room cabin in the canyon called fondly the Pump House, and Dad and his brothers took turns staying overnight down there once a week or so, pumping the reservoir full. One night, when it was Dad's turn and he was sleeping wth the pump-motor running, it malfunctioned, and filled the cabin with carbon monoxide. Somehow he woke up, very nearly asphyxiated, but managed to crawl outside, and so recovered. It had been a very close call, and thereafter the pump attendants slept outside when on duty.

Nobody in our family plied the moonshining trade during Prohibition (although my Uncle Stub built his legal career as a defender of moonshiners and never lost a case), but the canyon was almost certainly a haven for such operations. Like many another canyon hereabouts, it offered all the essentials: relative isolation, but close to town, running water, firewood, side-canyons for escape from revenuers. The risks were considerable—both legal and procedural: stills frequently exploded, or burned up, fueled by the spirits they were distilling. As a teenager I used to prowl every canyon I came to, hoping to find an intact still that my chums and I could restore and operate. But all I ever found were telltale lengths of coiled copper tubing, still attached to shattered husks of boilers, usually surrounded by charred hunks of wood—sure signs of somebody's on-the-job catastrophe.

The outbreak of World War Two brought significant though temporary changes to John Brown Canyon. The construction of a big army air base on the south end of Agency Plains meant that, by 1943, our hitherto friendly skies were full of fighter planes and bombers, roaring and zooming overhead day and night. Rumor had it that many of the flights were training exercises for top-secret low-level missions in Europe, taking advantage of our rugged terrain. Rumor or not, more than once we saw pairs of B-17 "Flying Fortresses" come charging out of the canyon, *below* the rims, their wing tips barely skimming the rimrocks, their roar rattling our windowpanes long after they were out of sight.

With such stimulations in the very air, as well as in the headlines and the newsreels (including news of the death in the Battle of Midway of John Campbell's younger brother George), my older brother and I and our schoolmates wasted no time in setting up the canyon as a key checkpoint in the defense of Jefferson County against invasion by the Japanese. Although we went on to build our ultimate fall-back fortification at New Era School a few miles to the north (as I have documented elsewhere), our military intuition told us that the Japanese invaders would surely use canyons like ours for their sneak attacks on the air base and Madras. So we labored feverishly after school and on weekends to construct a series of waist-high rimrock fortifications overlooking the creek bottom, supplemented by dizzy lookout platforms nailed into the branches of tall junipers.

If our parents knew what we were up to, they didn't let on, and so our intense contribution to what was called the War Effort went forward, heroically unheralded. "They also serve, who only stand and wait." Archaeologists of the future will probably identify our forts as sheep-folds, or Indian campsites, and that's probably just as well.

❧

COMING BACK INTO THE CANYON after a year's or even a season's absence is like rediscovering a fertile part of your mind that you've lost touch with.

As it happens, it's early summer, and the heat and glare on top have already penetrated partway down the steep canyon-sides, bringing out the greydiggers to chirp antiphonally on their rocks. "Digital! Digital! Digital!" is what they seem to be exclaiming, now that it's the twenty-first century. Although the meadowlarks never seem to descend into the depths of canyons like this one, I can hear them singing up on the rims, their songs at least three notes more elaborate and gleeful now than in winter.

As the sun angles over the slopes and the air begins to warm, I can smell the sharp canyon essence of juniper and sagebrush rising. The canyon-sides are so steep and close together here near the top that I can wave to my shadow-self on the other side, and he waves back cheerfully. I am following the "main trail" down, already re-inscribed this morning with the prints of a doe and a fawn, a coyote, and what looks like a rockchuck, or maybe a porcupine. Above and below the trail, an intricate net of game-trails covers the slope, as it always has, an image, maybe, of life's inbraided small possibilities, and how they add up to habitual patterns. Following them through their combinations, you could climb into and out of the canyon for a thousand years, and never follow quite the same route twice. In winter, dusted with snow, the game-trails look like a net of openwork lace thrown over the hillside.

Already the grasses are drying up for lack of rain, but just ahead I spy what may be the first mariposa lily bloom of the year, nodding blue-pink on its leafless stem. Supposedly, to pick a mariposa blossom is to cancel next year's flowering; I decline the gambit now, but know in my guilty heart that on the way out I'll not be able to resist plucking one for first show-and-tell bragging rights with my mother. It must run in the family, this urge to be the harbinger of seasonal returns; just last week, she reminded me that she and my father always vied for the honor of being the first to point out the new moon's slivery crescent to the other.

Further down, come July, the sandy slopes near the Pump House will suddenly be tricked out for a few weeks with blazing stars (*Mentzelia*), improbable but welcome in such a drab setting, with their big lemon-yellow flowers festooned with sepals, like dance-hall beauties in fancy hats passing through some frontier settlement. No point in picking a sample of *them*: they'll close up and wilt before you get them halfway home.

After one notably wet spring some years ago, there were stretches of this canyon-bottom cobbled every morning in June and on into July with meadow mushrooms, where none had ever appeared before. It was a coming-true of Robert Frost's great line about "the miracle of supply," and like Moses's people gathering manna in the desert, we felt obliged to harvest and eat them every day, until we were sick of the bounty—but still they kept on fruiting. Had the spores been in the ground all those years, waiting for the one good season in a lifetime? Or were they maybe imported from the mountain-meadows in the bowels of migrating deer? The next summer, no mushrooms, and they've never reappeared, but still I keep on looking.

Coming down now, I realize I'm half-expecting to meet someone walking up—odd, because in the old days such encounters almost never happened, the canyon was so unvisited. Even more so now, but still I'm imagining what it would be like, what I would say, if I met an Indian family setting out with their dogs for the Ochocos. Or John and Mattie Brown and their daughter, walking up to visit Whistling Smith. Or, on a Sunday hike, Harry Gard and his boys, who grew up out of this canyon to become war heroes, bank presidents, and politicians. Or Johnnie and Ella Campbell, strolling up to visit with my folks (something, I know well enough, that neither they nor we ever did). Or my dad, in his last year, slowly, painfully riding his old plug Blondie home after a day of trying to grub out poisonous water hemlocks, which he claimed "were taking the whole canyon." Even in broad daylight, it is a canyon full of friendly ghosts.

Now I'm down to the destination of many a family hike and innumerable picnics, the Sandstone Cliffs—great scarps of soft sandstone overladen with the basalt cliffs. There you can easily, irresistibly carve your initials with a jackknife or a nail—and for a hundred years people have duly registered their passages through the canyon, and paused to read the initials of their predecessors. Unlike graffiti sites in the city, there is a strict decorum in force here—initials only, and perhaps a date; no slogans, no greetings polite or rude. I've been tempted to go further with my knife, certainly, but wouldn't dare. But there's no rule against *repeating* your initials wherever you can find space on the rock, and so my dad's initials *A.S.R.* appear all over, often with those of his high school buddies *D.F.* and *H.H.,* dating to the 1920s; and my mother's *W.E.R.*, probably carved in her honor as she watched by Dad and later by my brother or me; and my brother's and mine, at different levels on the stone as we grew up; and now his wife's and kids' and mine, and so on into generations of Kilroy-Ramseys yet to be born, witnessing on soft sandstone our brief errands under these cliffs.

After a lifetime of such excursions, one comes to feel that they are necessary little pilgrimages, local rituals of return, deeply satisfying and reassuring in the way of such behavior, but lacking discovery and surprise. But not so, here at the Cliffs at least. A few years ago I was moping near them abreast of another outcropping of sandstone, in the same formation, and came upon a marvel: a child-sized human head and bust, carved out of the stone down to the shoulders, with jug ears and drilled-out eyes. If it ever had an expression, the face has been eroded into inscrutability; judging from the weathering, it must be as old as the homesteading era, but not I think the work of an Indian. Whoever did the carving, it must have taken him most of an afternoon, very different from the quick work of carving initials.

How had we familiars of the canyon, my brother and I and our friends, my dad and his, failed to discover this apparition, staring out sphinx-wise in his cliff-bottom alcove? I don't know, but maybe in an obscure place like this, *wonder* is somehow measured out to us, granted in increments, not all at once. Now when I ponder the canyon *in absentia,* I can't help conjuring up a Black man named John Brown and his fruit trees and cabbages down at its mouth, and our secretive sphinx here by the Sandstone Cliffs. And, because wonder doesn't want to be over and done with, I've begun to think again about a canyon adventure that somehow eluded me in my boyhood: to spend the night down here, on a certain grassy flat below these nominal cliffs, my bedroll protected against rattlesnakes within a loop of lasso-rope, under the rimrock slot of summer stars.

Eight

TWO HOMESTEADS

❖❖❖

YEARS AGO, AFTER LEARNING that all human productions are inescapably endowed with "style" by their creators, I resolved to attempt someday a comparative study of two things not often (if ever) formally compared. Namely, two ranches; specifically two homesteads east of Madras, Oregon—one, belonging to my family, called Sky Ranch, and the other, a couple of miles away, given various names over its one hundred twenty-year history, but here I'll call it by its original title, the OK Ranch. Maybe, I thought (not very seriously) if this study goes well, it might create a new academic field, of Comparative Ranch Studies. Why shouldn't it be at least as profitable to examine what ranchers make of their resources and ambitions, as to consider what novelists, or composers, or painters do with *theirs*?

But in truth I never carried this project beyond the woolgathering phase, until this book was nearing completion, and there seemed to be a place for it in my scheme of essays. So one day a couple of summers ago, while I was mending fences at the Sky Ranch, I resolved to walk over to the other place—across two deep draws and over two ridges—and revisit the OK, owned by absentee landlords and long since unoccupied, but still picturesque in the way of old upland ranches. I hadn't been over there for several years, and wanted to refresh my memory of the OK's distinctive farmstead geometry, and sharpen my sense of the differences between its layout and our place's.

But when I topped the second ridge and looked down, I knew, without immediately comprehending what I was seeing, that something was terribly wrong.

Most of the towering Lombardy poplars were gone. All of the barns, outbuildings, corrals, and rail-fences—gone. Where they had stood: what appeared to be building-sized ashpiles, white against the buckskin-colored dry grass.

I'd heard casual rumors that the old place was for sale again; it had even been listed in the *Wall Street Journal*. But whether the new owners had done this, or the old owners in a misguided effort to promote the

130

sale, I had no idea (I still don't), and it didn't matter, anyway. The OK Ranch as a kind of monument to clever homesteading, a place where the real ranching know-how was still on display, was simply gone: cut down, piled up, burnt to ashes, cleared off. Against my will I walked down to the place and moped around for an hour, until I'd found some scorched square nails and a bright blue enamel cookstove ash-door as keepsakes to carry away.

It's a little wonder of inertia and benign neglect, of course, that this hadn't happened long before, say after the original homesteader's son-in-law sold the place in the early 1950s. At least, I consoled myself, whatever the new owners decide to do with it, we have photographs and memories of how it once looked. But something precious, old and enduring and expressive of human ingenuity and skill, had been subtracted from the landscape. So, unexpectedly, my comparative study of two old out-of-the-way places has taken on an elegiac aspect, at least for the OK Ranch.

❖

BOTH OF THESE PLACES STRADDLE the climatological boundary between the typical sagebrush and juniper terrain of the central Oregon range country, and the pine- and fir-covered foothills of the Ochoco Mountains, a western extension of the Blue Mountains of eastern Oregon. This boundary is so sharply defined up here it looks almost human-made, as if it were the result of logging along a hillside line marking an altitude of 4,500 feet, precisely where the clouds, having dropped their moisture on the Cascade Range on their way east, have become moist enough again to unload some rain and snow on these hills. The average yearly precipitation is about twenty inches; hence the evergreens and other living signs of a subalpine zone—Oregon grape, camas, grass widows and blue flax, shooting stars. The Sky Ranch is almost equally divided between these two zones; the OK is mostly on the upland, forested side of the boundary.

Both places lie hard against Blizzard Ridge, a weather-maker to the north; and if you wanted to tell some outlander where to find them, you would begin by saying that they are both above the eastern edge of Hay Creek Basin. Now Hay Creek Ranch has figured on most maps of central Oregon since the 1870s, rightly so; through many owners it has been the dominant social and economic force in these parts since its establishment in 1873 by Dr. D. W. Baldwin. It's doubtful that either the OK or the Sky Ranch or any other homesteads in "Hay Creek country" would have survived for long, without the facilities and human presence of the big ranch.

In its heyday in the first decades of the twentieth century, under the direction of an English aristocrat, John Griffith Edwards, Hay Creek Ranch covered well over a hundred thousand acres, and its huge flocks of sheep (up to forty thousand) and cattle grazed on unclaimed government land as well as on the ranch properties. Beginning with the Merino flocks of his predecessor, Dr. Baldwin, J. G. Edwards developed a Merino/Rambouillet/Delaine cross of large, heavy-fleeced animals that became famous as the "Baldwin sheep," with sheep ranchers coming from around the world to buy breeding stock. In the 1920s the ranch sold a sizable lot of breeding animals to the Russian government, and two Hay Creek regulars—Frank Gill and Clayton Garrett—actually "herded" the flock all the way, first by train to the East Coast, and then by ship to St. Petersburg. Unfortunately, when the sheep were being unloaded there, hungry peasants rioted (there was another Russian famine underway), and carried them off to be eaten.

For ordinary homesteaders around the Hay Creek Ranch in the 1880-1920 era, it was an indispensable source of occasional and full-time employment, and it served most of the purposes of a town, with a post office, commissary, and medical supplies available. Most of its owners and managers have kept up a "good neighbor" policy that is part of its unwritten history, and to this day the ranch generously anchors its sparsely populated territory.

In the early days of settlement, up to about the outbreak of World War One, the town of commerce and record for this area was Prineville, about twenty-five miles to the south around Grizzly Mountain; but after Jefferson County was carved out of Crook County's north flank in 1914, the new county seat, Madras (fifteen miles due west, over the Baldwin Hills), became the main market town and railroad terminus. There was a closer settlement, Ashwood, but its glory-days as a mining town had played out well before the Great Depression, and the road to it from Hay Creek country was a vehicular horror year-round.

Who were the homesteaders and tumbleweeds who found their way into the Hay Creek country and at least briefly took up land, starting in the 1880s and peaking just before World War One? The evidence suggests that on the whole they were not like the hard-headed dirt farmers (a lot of them from Missouri) who homesteaded on the north, south, and east sides of Madras in the first decade of the new century. Instead, the settlers out by Hay Creek and beyond were a decidedly mixed population, with very diverse backgrounds and motives for homesteading. But it's fair to say that for many of them, farming was only one reason for trying to claim free acres; and with Hay Creek already occupying most of the best land for tillage and pasturage, they mostly accepted the alternative of subsistence farming. The main thing seems to have been to set up to live the best way you could and enjoy the magnificent surroundings while you were there.

Their economies varied, of course: most kept sheep, some attempted cattle and horses; the wives and children sold chicken and eggs in Madras; there was some small-scale logging, especially early on; and nearly everybody who could do it cut and delivered firewood and juniper fenceposts to the lowland farmers. During Prohibition, of course, nearly every lonely canyon and draw up here had its moonshine still, served by fleets of wily runners and distributors who plied the risky routes between between Supply and Demand.

There were, to be sure, would-be entrepreneurs, like Edwin A. Allen who named his place (just west of the Sky Ranch) the Diamond A, and for a few years maintained a diversified operation including a dairy, a sawmill, and a custom threshing outfit. But what really counts in Ed Allen's story is that he always claimed that he originally saw the Diamond A in a dream, while living in Iowa, and so searched through the West until he found the real place of his dreams in central Oregon. Brigham Young, who overlooked the Valley of the Salt Lake and proclaimed, "This is the place!", would have understood such a visonary recognition.

A surprising number of the "entrymen" (and women) up here were from the East, with good educations and informed tastes. When we bought Tom and Evada Power's place in 1945, in the attic we found boxes of issues of a magazine that struck us then as truly exotic: the *New Yorker*, each issue addressed to "T. and E. Power, Hay Creek, Oregon." Tom was a Newfoundlander with family connections in Boston; Evada had literary aspirations, and in later years wrote features on local history for the Redmond *Spokesman*.

An early neighbor of theirs, Victor Shawe (whose brother Bruce, also a homesteader, taught at the Fairview School on the Powers' property), eventually left his homestead for other, more worldly pursuits, but in the 1920s turned his homesteading experiences to good acount as a short-story writer of national prominence. Between 1920 and 1928 he published more than a dozen stories in the *Saturday Evening Post*—most of them vividly set in the country between Blizzard Ridge and Grizzly Mountain.

Before leaving central Oregon for Idaho (where he eventually became secretary to the governor) Victor Shawe served as superintendent of schools in Crook County, and it's an intriguing guess that in that capacity he might have known another central Oregon homesteader/teacher/writer, Alice Day Pratt. Her place was in the Paulina country south of Prineville and thus out of our territory, but we're talking here about why such people took up sagebrush homesteads. Alice Pratt, a single woman from the Midwest, filed on 160 acres near Maury Mountain in 1912, and by the time she finally sold her beloved Broadview on the eve of the Depression, it covered a full section of range-pasture and fields, and she had launched her literary career with an extraordinary book about her life on the range, *The Homesteader's Portfolio*. Re-settled in New York City, she went on to write two popular children's books, both drawing on her years in central Oregon: *Animals of a Sagebrush Ranch,* and *Animal Babies*.

Pratt and Shawe did ultimately move beyond their ranching lives in Oregon, but like many others here, they seem to have taken up homesteading mainly because it allowed them to live where, and how, they wanted to live. It still seems like a romantic, or perhaps a Thoreauvian, notion, as it clearly did for one of those who stayed, Tom Power, when he looked back over forty years on his land:

> The place fulfilled a city dweller's dream of independence.
> It was situated at the foot of the Blue Mountains, with a
> western view of the Cascades, and sometimes thirteen
> snow-covered peaks plainly visible. I decided to become a
> homesteader. There was grass and water in abundance, with
> fairly level fields just waiting for the plow. I became,
> indeed, "lord of all that I survey." Although it wasn't as
> easy as it sounded, I have never regretted my decision. I
> have found health, the one thing I lacked when I lived in a
> crowded city. I have found peace of mind and happiness
> and a modicum of this world's goods in Central Oregon.
>
> (*Jefferson County Reminiscences*)

❧

Now with this much as background, let's focus on the OK Ranch and the Sky Ranch, originally Tom Power's Tee Pee, and try to align them for comparison.

When John D. and Mary O'Kelley filed on high land north of Blizzard Ridge, they were (like most of the region's homesteaders-to-come) well-traveled. According to family tradition, they were the first couple to be married in the frontier town of Lakeview (in 1877); then they moved to Paisley in the heart of the Oregon high desert, where their first child, Leona, was born—the first white child born in Paisley.

In the middle 1880s they moved further north to Prineville, where John O'Kelley operated a blacksmith shop, but the violence and vigilante justice of the town in those days drove them further north yet, to the mining town of Ashwood. Again, it wasn't the right place, so in 1889 they determined to load up their wagon and strike out once again, this time all the way to California. But the site of their very first night's camp, at a spring just below timberline south of Blizzard Ridge, looked so promising that they reconsidered on the spot—"this is the place."

In the recollections of their youngest daughter, Birdie, "Father rode to Prineville, filed on the place as a homestead. They built up the place, planted lots of trees, lived there for 19 years." When Birdie O'Kelley Palmateer was in her eighties, she wrote part of her life's story and gave it to a friend, Martha Stranahan, and I don't know of a more compelling account of growing up in this country in those early days. Birdie's adult life seems to have been uncommonly hardscrabble and full of disappointments (although she did gain some local fame as a lariat artist at rodeos), so maybe her recollections of an idyllic childhood on the OK are selective and a little colored with nostalgia. I doubt it—but judge for yourself.

> The first years of my life was wonderful, growing up in that beautiful place, with timber nearby, lots of bunch grass, wildflowers of every kind on the hills. We children would put in hours gathering wildflowers and picking up pretty rocks. Nowadays the rocks are called agates and fire opals. To us they were just rocks.
>
> There were all kinds of wild animals which we saw occasionally.
>
> My father ran horses over the range—had around 300 head. In the last years of the ranch he also had 50 or 60

cattle, some hogs, chickens, and a vegetable garden which we had to take care of.

We children had saddle horses and saddles, and rode many miles over the hills. We had to ride seven miles to the Post Office at Hay Creek Ranch for our mail. I made my first trip alone at age seven. My father wanted a letter mailed and said if there was a letter for him with a certain address to hurry back with it, so in three hours I was back—14 miles round-trip. He said it was a good time, as I had four gates to open and close both ways, and a sucking colt following who would run down the fence instead of going through the gate when I took the mare through. I'd have to chase him to get back with his mother.

My sister Martina and I would go for the mail about every two weeks, bring back all the neighbors' mail, usually about two fifty-pound flour-sacks full, *Oregon Journal, Oregon Farmer, Hearth and Home*, and a few other oldtime magazines.

My sister Georgina liked to cook and sew. Brother Bart was usually helping in the fields.

We had two three-month school [terms], three [months] in the spring, three in the fall, so the children could help their parents in the summer, and there was too much snow in the winter. The teacher got $30 per month, boarded with some of the directors for free. When we'd get home from school, which was 1 1/2 miles away [further up Blizzard Ridge] we would change our dresses and go to hunt the cows. Sometimes they would be with Hay Creek cattle and we'd be afraid, so we would send an old cow dog after them. He would separate them and head them home.

We would get the calves in from the calf pasture. They would take part of the milk and we would help Mother milk the rest. We carried it to a nice sawdust cellar where it was strained into pans. A couple of days later we'd skim the cream off into the churn. Milk would be carried to the hogs. t was usually my job to churn. Sometimes we'd have eight to ten pounds of butter per churning. Mother would take care of that, mold it into pound molds, sell it to the Hay Creek Co. for fifteen cents a pound, eggs ten cents per dozen.

When the sheep at Hay Creek lambed there would be some lambs the ewes wouldn't claim or they would have twins, and not enough milk. They would give them to us girls. We would go on horseback with grain-sacks. We would cut holes in the sacks, put the little lambs in, and hang them over the saddle horn to take them home and raise them. They were known as "bummers." We would raise them up to 70-80 pounds and sell them for $3 to $5 per head. We always got new calico dress material for our work, the material was only 8 cents a yard, new hair ribbons for 25 cents, and mother took the rest of the money and bought us shoes and whatever else we needed for winter.

Sometimes my father broke and matched up a team to sell. We would have to raise a colt from one of the mares, feed him milk two or three times a day. If you went out with a pan and it wasn't for the colt, he would wheel and kick at you—some of them got pretty mean …

When I was 10 years old [1908] my happy days began to fade. My father sold the old home place, and moved to Culver, where he rented 1200 acres of wheat land from George Rodman. He ran that place for two years, had several hired men, also bought a J. I. Case threshing machine. He threshed for lots of people, including new settlers in the Opal City, Redmond, Powell Butte, and Sisters areas. When I was 14 we moved to Redmond. My father sold the ranch and threshing machine …Later my folks decided to move to Silver Lake, where the government was opening up some homestead land.

"We were free as the wind" is how my great-aunt Hazel McCoin liked to describe how it was when she visited her cousin Birdie at the OK Ranch, when they were little girls, nearly a century ago. They could ride all day without seeing anyone; usually one of their horses was a mare with a sucking colt, as Aunt Hazel remembered it, and when they grew thirsty they would jump off, shoo the colt away, and drink warm mare's milk. Like regular little Cossacks; no wonder Birdie cherished such memories of freedom in her later life as a hard-pressed wife and mother.

About the farmstead itself, she notes, in passing, that her parents "built up the place, [and] planted lots of trees ..."—an understatement, even in terms of what remained of the OK fifty or even ten years ago, before its demolition. From every angle, in large details and small, you saw evidence of careful, savvy planning and construction; all the parts seemed to fit together, and for farming purposes at least, form followed function ingeniously and elegantly. If it's possible to say that a rough upland homestead can have real style, the OK did.

The many trees Birdie mentions included a huge L-shaped windbreak of Lombardy poplars (probably started from cuttings from the even older Parrish Place below Hay Creek headquarters). The long leg of the L ran east and west, to provide a barrier against the north wind that roars off Blizzard Ridge (which John O'Kelley named) with the short leg at the west end providing some protection from west winds up from Hay Creek Basin. What was protected was a triple row of fruit trees—apples, pears, and prunes—still bearing a little fruit until the place was cleared off.

The house—a three-story structure, with a big front porch facing east, where the road passed—was in some cottonwoods on the top of the L. It may be that the house was improved upon after the O'Kelleys left in 1908, but the evidence of good original design was obvious, including piped-in, fauceted water (from an excellent spring up the draw) and plenty of window-light in the rooms. The inside walls were all covered with wallpaper, over newspapers glued to the bare boards, where Birdie and her family might have read headline stories in the San Francisco *Chronicle* about the Spanish-American War. Just behind the house was a dug-out building with double log walls filled with sawdust, clearly the cellar/ice house where Birdie remembered storing milk, cream, and butter.

But it was out in the farmyard proper that the OK's elegantly functional style really expressed itself. It was laid out on a flat stretch of land, well above the creek, allowing for good drainage. The barn and outbuildings were built close to each other, clearly to make working in and around them more efficient, especially in hard weather. The big old barn, which was leaning dramatically southward when I last saw it (after a century of fronting the north wind), was placed squarely in the center of the farmyard. The pole rafters over its capacious haymow had been roofed with hand-split shakes, probably made on the ranch, or else at the Durham Mill a few miles to the east. Access to the haymow, whether by pitchfork or some sort of hay-derrick, was gained through swing-doors on several levels in the north wall; as soon as hay piled up to one door's

level, the next door would be opened, and so on until the mow was filled
with the year's hay crop. (There were hayfields scattered all over the
place, especially south across the creek from the headquarters.) On the
barn's west side were mangers and calf-pens, where hay from the mow
could be pitchforked down with a minimum of effort to feed the stock.

Just east of the barn, the O'Kelleys built their post-and-pole corrals—
a large square one and, connected to it by a gate at one corner, a classical
round corral for breaking and training horses. The former was provided
with an unusually large dugout trough, hewn out of pine or fir, at least
two feet in diameter and looking like the beginnings of a Haida war-
canoe. It was kept filled from a standpipe connected to the spring up
the draw.

The last resident of the place, Jim Garrett (the O'Kelley's son-in-law),
was a notable horse trainer, and in the late 1940s, we asked him to keep
and work with a promising young sorrel mare we owned, named
(inevitably) Flicka. He did wonders with her—she came back to us a first-
class cutting horse; and although both Jim and Flicka, his pupil, are long
gone, I like to think about them working together slowly, easily, *patiently*,
inside the round corral, going over the lessons of separating cows and
holding the calf-rope tight but not too tight.

Just west of the barn stood a combination granary/pighouse, its upper
story for storing feed and grain (I'm sure there was a gristmill down on
the creek, but have never found signs of it), and the ground floor for
hogs, with a human-door and a hog-door in opposite walls. Connecting
the two floors were several vertical chutes, which emptied on the pig-
level into feedbins, making it easy (and sanitary) to keep the porkers in
feed. The pig-sized hatch on the ground floor led directly to a depression
in the ground, perpetually muddy from overflow water from the horse
trough—a wallow no hog could find fault with.

Where the OK chicken house stood, I don't know; likewise, I've never
figured out the location of the vegetable garden, or John O'Kelley's
blacksmith shop. We know from his daughter's memoir that he had been
a blacksmith in Prineville, and there used to be evidence of his forging
skills all over the place: gate-post pivot-bearings fashioned from old
wagon-wheel hubs; door-hinges forged from whatever was handy; and
handmade latches everywhere.

One particular form of these latches has always symbolized for me the
ingenious style of the whole place. Horses are often smart enough to learn
how to use their noses and teeth to unlock almost any gate (especially if

it leads on to hay or grain)—that, in fact, was one bad habit that Jim Garrett wasn't able to drill out of our mare Flicka. But it wouldn't have been a problem around the OK Ranch, anyway. All the critical doors in the barn and granary were latched from the *inside*—with a round hole in each door just big enough for a human hand to reach in and lock or unlock the latch. If this isn't an artful solution to a real-world problem, I don't know what is—and it typifies the way the OK Ranch was set up and operated by the O'Kelleys and their successors the Garretts.

IN 1911, THREE YEARS AFTER the O'Kelley family moved off the OK and Birdie O'Kelley's girlhood idyll on the ranch came to an end, a young man with a peculiar accent filed a claim on some land a couple of miles to the south, not far west of Big Sheep Rock. His name was Tom Power; he'd grown up on Bell Island, near St. Johns, Newfoundland, and after several years of knocking about, most recently in the Yukon, he arrived in central Oregon just ahead of the railroads, grubstaked with Alaska gold and eager to find himself a homestead. After some fruitless searching with a hired "locator," he was about to give up on the area and move on, when an old settler showed him a place in the hills about six miles east of the Hay Creek Ranch headquarters.

The land centered on a good year-round spring at the lower end of a draw between two hills on the south and the east. There was evidence of previous occupation—someone had planted a row of poplars, and there was a fallen-in shack dug into the foot of the eastern hill. It was squatter's work; in the Crook County Courthouse in Prineville, Tom found no prior claim to the site and the 160 acres he wanted, so he filed his claim and went to work building a cabin and then opening up and fencing fields wherever he could find reasonably flat ground. Not an easy task, in such hilly terrain, but the soil was black and relatively rock free.

After a few months he received a letter, which unpleasantly cleared up the mystery of the place's previous occupant, the squatter. It was sent from the Oregon State Prison in Salem, written by an inmate named "Dick Turpin" (not his real name: his family still lives in central Oregon), who evidently had used the place as a hideout in his cow-and-horse-thieving operations, and now threatened Tom with violent harm if he didn't get off the land. Tom wrote back, offering him a hundred dollars for his improvements on the place, but Turpin replied refusing the offer and threatening to take the property back by force upon his release. Soon afterward he wrote once again (this would have been in 1912) saying that he was now out of prison, and setting a deadline for Tom to be off the place, or else.

But Tom stood his ground. The deadline passed, months went by, and he had almost forgotten the threats, when one day a stranger showed up just at sunset. He said he was Dick Turpin, apologized for the threatening letters, called himself a fool for not accepting the hundred dollars—and then asked if he could just spend one last night at the place he'd loved. Not surprisingly, Tom refused the request and sent him on his way.

Judging from newspaper records, what had happened was that after getting out of prison on parole, Turpin and one of his accomplices had gotten themselves arrested again, for stealing cattle over on Trout Creek and trying to sell the meat, and been sent back to the "Pen" for violating parole and then released pending appeal of their original conviction. Apparently it was in this interval of freedom that he called on Tom, perhaps from a sincere desire to see "his" place once more; perhaps in a dubious attempt to win Tom's sympathy as a possible character witness; perhaps for more sinister motives. Whatever the reasons for his visit, Dick Turpin lost his appeal, and went back to prison to serve an extended sentence, never to reappear at his old hideout. As a child, going to sleep under the poplars he'd planted, I used to imagine I could hear his ghost calling in their branches.

In later years an accomplished storyteller in the style of his Irish and Newfie forebears, Tom Power was full of such tales about his adventures as a young homesteader. A few, like this one, he wrote down, but most vanished into breath, as stories will, unless someone tries to listen to them for more than the momentary pleasure of the telling. The Powers had no children, no local relatives, and I was too young when I was around him to know what I would be missing, someday, for lack of attention.

One of his favorite yarns should be read in its entirety, as he wrote it out for a book of local history, *Jefferson County Reminiscences,* but I can only summarize it here. That same year of his showdown with Dick Turpin, he had another Wild West encounter—with some angry Indians from the Warm Springs Reservation, who were accustomed to traveling through what was now his place, on their way to hunting grounds further east. Seeing an Indian woman walking near the cabin, he called out to her, asking if she had any buckskin gloves to sell. But she ran off, as if in a fright.

A little later, while he was up on the cabin's roof, shingling it, an Indian man appeared with a knife, and angrily accused him of assaulting his wife the day before. After a heated exchange, Tom finally persuaded the outraged husband that he wasn't the villain; probably it was a sheepherder who'd been around the neighborhood. As the Indian walked off, Tom looked around and saw eight or nine more Indians coming out of the trees behind the house, all holding rifles. A little later, a mixed-blood who was traveling with the band came over the hill to see what was happening, and Tom gave him a stern message to take back:

> I said to the half-breed, "The Indians came very near
> making a great mistake, and I will not allow Indians to
> camp on my place. Tell them I will give them one hour to
> move, and you will also tell them never to come on my
> place again!" I showed him the lines and he hastened to the
> camp with my orders. And that has held good to the
> present day. A trail they formerly used was abandoned and
> they go around my place.—*Jefferson County Reminiscences*

In Tom's telling, this hair-raising adventure ran right into another one, and there's really nothing for it but to let him tell this one in his own words. All things considered, it must have been an anxious first year on the place!

> I walked over to tell the old carpenter [a neighbor] my
> experience [with the Indians] that evening, and he was
> quite concerned. He urged me to stay with him as I had
> neither doors nor windows in place. I felt that I should not
> give in to the first fear that came my way. As I got closer to
> the cabin I realized that I should have followed his advice.
> It was the fall of the year and I could plainly hear someone
> walking on the fallen leaves that surrounded my cabin.
> Crunch, crunch, and then quiet, and then a few more
> steps, around and around my cabin. To be sure I thought
> the Indians had come back to kill me.
>
> When the footsteps stopped I crawled forward on my
> hands and knees to get a better view, as the moon came up
> from behind the hill. [I was] so intent in my scouting of
> the cabin before me, and my ears keyed to the faintest
> sound, that I had forgotten about the caved-in cellar [Dick

Turpin's work]. I raised up to get as better view, and as I took a step forward I stepped off the bank into the cellar. I landed on the back of an old cow who was lying there. She was as frightened as I was. She gave a loud bellow and then her tail went up over her back and she lost no time in getting to her feet. Before I had a chance to realize what was happening, she was running away with me. When she stopped long enough for me to fall off she had carried me nearly two miles. Was I mad? The old cow had made the footsteps that had raised my hair in fear.—*Jefferson County Reminiscenses*

One wonders—assuming that Tom was corresponding with his family back in Newfoundland at this time—what they made of such amazing episodes on the Frontier. Many years later, in the 1950s, he went all the way home to Bell Island for a visit, and subsequently wrote a charming memoir of his boyhood there. But alas, although the memoir is full of tales of childhood misdeeds and mishaps, he doesn't connect them with his subsequent adventures in Oregon, or digress on how his Newfoundland upbringing prepared him for homesteading on the range. All he offers on that score is an acknowledgment that the skills with knots he learned from sailors back home on the Atlantic shore had served him well on the ranch, and a brief tribute to the noble Newfoundland dog, which, he assures us, he kept in Oregon.

Maybe, knowledge of knots and dogs apart, he simply had to make up his new homesteading career as he went, impromptu, trial by error and trial again, as many of his tenderfoot contemporaries in Central Oregon had to do; as skillful John O'Kelley over the hill obviously did *not*. The fact of the matter is that the *style* of the Power place when we bought it thirty-five years later had a decidedly improvised, ad hoc quality to it, in both large and small details. The contrast between its casual organization of parts, and the integrated design of the OK Ranch, was striking, and fascinating. Where the OK outbuildings had their elegant horse-proof door latches, the Tee Pee doors were more or less secured on the outside by crude toggles of wood, each pivoting on a nail to open or lock the door—until the nail-hole wore loose around the nail, and you had to hammer the nail in tighter, if you could.

The farmstead site itself afforded the crucial advantage of dependable water from the spring just up the draw. But there was no "view," at least not from the house itself; the hills immediately to the east and south seem to close in, especially in dark weather. Now I'm pretty sure that Tom Power and indeed most homesteaders up here would have hooted at the notion of seeking "view property," holding that "view"—west to the Cascades, for example—was a reward for getting out and walking your lands, not something you sought to enjoy from your front steps or parlor.

But from an "operational" standpoint, the Tee Pee *was* disadvantageous, or at least awkward; the land tilts, and slopes, every which way. Tom never attempted a barn; the two-room granary had to be built up on stilts on its lower end, and has been leaning downhill ever since its beams and planks were green lumber. The long low lambing sheds, open to the east for solar warmth and shelter from the west winds, straggled up the slopes south of the granary, and eventually collapsed down the same incline. The upper half of the corrals is almost level, but the lower half plunges eastward over a steep incline right down to the bottom of the draw above the house, where there was water for a trough. Needless to say, the corral posts and poles lean as gravity dictates. In truth, the pines and junipers are the only things plumb and perpendicular hereabouts.

The outhouse, perched a short distance up the eastern hillside from the back door of the house, gradually leaned further and further into its slope, until it seemed to some in our extended family to be in danger of toppling clear over, like some rustic leaning Tower of Privy. Finally, when using it became too thrilling for comfort, we dug a new hole down on flatter ground, and skidded the whole shack down the hill to its new site, where it should last for at least another century. Up here, following Tom Power's precedents, we wouldn't have thought of building a new one.

The overall effect of the place is, well, picturesque, as if the artist who drew the old cowboy cartoon strip in the funny papers, "Red Ryder and Little Beaver," had used the Tee Pee as inspiration for his ramshackly ranch settings. But everything worked, more or less, and still works. The fences are irregular and uneven in quality, to put it mildly, but still stand their ground, mostly; the gates still open and close, but sag as they probably did from the beginning. A tin roof, a new water line from the spring, the new-old outhouse, and some interior mouse-proofing in the house are about the extent of our improvements on the Tee Pee, since we made it the Sky Ranch. A tradition, a style continues: let the facilities be as good as they need to be, but no better than. And, the OK and a few other places around here excepted, that's been the general norm for these uphill homesteads.

It's not that the Powers lacked ambition, or a sense of community. Living frugally, building up a decent herd of cattle (the brand was TAP) and a band of sheep, they were willing and able to buy out adjoining lands as their neighbors starved out and gave up in the twenties. Even before his marriage to Evada, Tom was civic-minded enough to donate some of his most level land, on a bench below the house, for a school, and helped build the schoolhouse, proudly known as "Fairview School." Until the school closed in the late 1930s, most of Fairview's teachers boarded with the Powers. Remarkably, the twelve hundred acres that constituted the ranch when we bought it comprised *nine* separate holdings besides Tom's original 160-acre claim. Their owners (with names long gone from this country) were:

William West
David and Polly Gay
Mary Gay (their daughter, "a single woman")
Charles Brammer
Richard Winslow
Bruce Shawe
Gus and Elizabeth Kibbee
Horace Kibbee
Mrs. Kibbee (their mother)

The Kibbee land, which the Powers bought in 1928, lies in the timber one ridge east of the Power house. Gus Kibbee and his family, and his bachelor brother Horace (a journalist and printer by trade), and their mother were well established on their homesteads by the time Tom arrived in 1911. Gus planted a lovely little orchard by his farmstead on Kibbee Creek, and had irrigation rights on the creek, apparently for a truck garden. His first cousin was the celebrated character actor Guy Kibbee, featured in hundreds of silent and talkie films in the twenties, thirties, and forties, and best known for playing shrewd but lovable codgers, as in the "Scattergood Baines" series. He also played St. Peter in Jack Benny's movie *The Horn Blows at Midnight*, and often went on theatrical tours throughout the West, in the course of which it's more than likely that he visited Gus and his family up here, about as far from Hollywood glare and glitter as you could get.

Judging from photos, the Kibbee house was impressive: three stories, with a full-length porch facing the creek. My mother has always wondered why, when they bought the Kibbee place, Tom and Evada didn't just vacate their little cabin over the hill and move into the much roomier and tighter Kibbee house, fronted as it was on three sides by lovely meadows and the willow-lined creek. Instead, Tom tore the house down for the lumber, but did salvage the entire front porch, which he somehow grafted onto the front of his own house. It was and is still the old building's one embellishment, with beautifully groined rafters, and he was very proud of it. To be sure, the porch floor has tilted for years because he didn't get a proper foundation under it—but still, screened-in in front and on the sides, and shaded by Dick Turpin's ancient poplars, it's the best place in the world for an indoor picnic on a hot day, or a conversation on a rainy one.

My father loved to tell about his first visit to the place with Tom, when he was thinking about buying it. This would have been in 1944; Tom had been elected judge of Jefferson County just before the war, and he and Evada had taken an apartment in Madras, and were staying at the ranch only when time and weather (and gas rationing) allowed. So it was not surprising to find evidence, as they walked in the door, that packrats and mice had begun, in the owners' absence, to move in. But when Tom and Dad entered the kitchen, and found rat debris and mouse-turds all over the sink-counter, Tom merely remarked, "Well, Gus, we'll just have to reclaim some space here and set up for a meal!" And so saying, he swept the rodent clutter to the floor with a lordly sweep of his arm, and took down the frying pan! It was an altogether typical gesture; as the Irish like to say, he was an *easy* man.

On their next trip (I think the sale was already confirmed), I was allowed to come along, age about seven. Before getting down to business with Dad, whatever it was, Tom led me out into the front yard. There, partly covered with leaves, was a heap of small rocks as tall as I was. "Now then," he said, "these are treasure-rocks the wife and I have brought in over the years. Why don't you go through them and take what you like? This one's a 'thunder egg'—might have quartz or even agate inside. Here's a hammer to crack it open with." Cracking thunder eggs all that day, and reflecting that this place we were buying was full of mineral wonders, and springs and creeks and mysterious old buildings too, I could hardly contain myself. And that initial enchantment has never faded.

❖❖

WHAT CAN WE CONCLUDE FROM OUR RAGGED COMPARISON of the OK and the Tee Pee-cum-Sky Ranch? The *irony* of the two cases is brutally plain: the one place masterfully laid out and built, but then in later years neglected, unused, and ultimately demolished, leaving only an old woman's brief memoir of her childish happiness there; the other place sort of cobbled together from the start, no better than it had to be in any detail, but somehow cherished, frequented, and preserved for almost a century now. There was love and pride in each homesteader's enterprise, surely—the "elegant solutions" of the OK attest to more than just skill in John O'Kelley's founding of his place, notwithstanding his abrupt leaving of it for other prospects. And maybe the very looseness of the Powers' stewardship of *their* place expresses their love for it. If so, it was a love based not so much on material cultivation and improvement, as on spiritual occupation: living where and how they wanted to live. "This is the place." Reflecting now on my own family's tenure on the Tee Pee/ Sky Ranch, now almost twice as long as the Powers' stay, and acknowledging that we've taken one good wheat crop, several loggings, and many generations of fat cattle off the place, it still feels like a spiritual legacy—something we didn't buy from Tom and Evada Power, but rather inherited from them, with the wayward and splintery old buildings, the unchanging skylines, and the ever-changing sky.

When you come onto a place where time mainly shows itself in the weathering of old boards and the rusting of iron, and the perpetual succession of wildflowers, always new on the hillsides, what is there to improve?

THE LAST TIME I TOOK MY FATHER up to the Sky Ranch, only a month or so before his death, we had a fine day of it, in clear mild weather, and he got to reminiscing, that sternly sentimental man, about the good times we'd enjoyed up here. As we started home, passing through the front gate, his name on the sign, he leaned back and said in a voice I seemed to be overhearing, "You know, if I could start again, be a young man again, I'd try to find myself some old place, just below the timber, one or two good springs, and just carry on with cows and calves, and hay. Now wouldn't that be a life?" Looking back, he could see, *This was that world; it was all here, his dream: time was all it wanted.*

Nine

AN IMPROMPTU ON OWNING LAND

❖❖

I OWN SOME LAND, IN THE WESTERN FOOTHILLS of the Ochoco Mountains in central Oregon. Somewhere or other I have a packet of papers indicating that I have title to it. I pay yearly county taxes on this property; if I stop paying them, the county will claim the property, and eventually auction it off "for back taxes," which is exactly how my parents bought our home-place at the end of the Depression. So we pay taxes on what we own.

Actually, I hold joint-title to this foothill property with my brother and our wives. It's understood in this arrangement that we share it equally, undividedly, right down to the smallest indivisible unit, an acre, a square foot, a grain of sand. What's ours is theirs, and vice versa. No problem there, because we're close; but most of the time, when I think about the place, or walk around it, it's as if I'm the owner, and I imagine my brother thinks of it in the same way. When the place makes us a little money, on timber or pasture-rental, we share equally, and likewise the expenses of keeping it up.

This easy arrangement is going to become more complicated, I think, when the place passes on to my brother's children and their spouses, and my three children and theirs. Can ten or twelve owners carry on as easily as four, pay the taxes, keep the fences and the old farmhouse in repair, resist the temptations to "develop" and make deals? I worry that possession of the place will not mean to all of them what it means to this generation. And in the *next* generation, after them ... ? Maybe we should form a "family corporation" now, so that conflicts-to-come can be settled, even by buy-outs if need be. But that seems awfully drastic, even dynastic, for an old worn-out sheep-ranch that up to now has been maintained by a kind of neglectfully possessive love.

When my father bought the place almost sixty years ago, from the original homesteader, the latter (who had mined for gold in the Yukon) insisted on retaining the mineral rights. A strange feature of Oregon law is that mineral rights can be perpetually separated from real property rights, so now, after all these years, I'm not really sure who holds the former. It may be a dentist in San Diego, who probably doesn't know what he owns up here. It's a serious vexation; I couldn't show you where our real property rights end, and his mineral rights begin, but if he suddenly found the deed to our place and decided to prospect on it for oil and natural gas, he could come through our gates willy-nilly, and set up drilling rigs wherever he pleased on an acre of ground for each well, and drill as deep as he wanted, using our water as necessary! Who would ever think of dividing land up that way? My dad must have wanted the place very badly, to have accepted such a deal. I hope it doesn't turn around and bite us one of these days.

Thinking about those buried, alienated minerals, I brood sometimes about the air over my property. Do I own it; how much? Probably about as high as I can reach up and fan with my hat, no more. Maybe I should test this assumption by erecting a three hundred-foot flagpole and flying a proprietary flag on it. But for all intents and purposes I've conceded that what I own, really, is the gritty mineral skin of the land, which I share with ants and lizards, sagebrush and trees, and enough air and sunshine for all of us to live. When it rains, I get to keep what soaks in. Fair enough.

Long before it was homesteaded the place was visited by Paiute and probably Chinookan Indians on hunting and root-gathering expeditions. I doubt that they settled in for long, up here, although we still find their arrowheads and hide-scrapers, especially on sandy south-facing hillsides, where they could make sun-warmed camps. Once I found the bottom of a very old bottle: the glass, sun-blued and full of bubbles, had been expertly chipped to make a sharp scraping edge. That would date it around 1860, at the latest. Did the Indians who came up here then or before think this stretch of country "belonged" to them? No more than they would have claimed any other parcel they regularly traveled through. More likely, so far as they reflected on it at all, they held that the land owned *them*, as a mother owns her children, and so they possessed the freedom and the duties of being owned; that would have been the basis of their allegiance.

As late as the 1920s, Indians from the Warm Springs Reservation used to ride up here in the fall, with their kids, pack horses, and dogs, and camp in the willows along one of our creeks. Probably they were on their way to hunt deer and elk in the Ochoco Mountains further east and south, but they would stay long enough here to build and use sweat lodges in the willows. A very old lady who grew up on this part of our place told me this years ago, just before she died. She remembered that her father always welcomed them onto his land, and usually traded whatever he had to offer for buckskin gloves and moccasins. She also remembered that her family's neighbor over the hill, who ended up owning both properties before we bought all of it, had some trouble with the Indians early on and told them never to come on his place, and they didn't.

This meant, I guess, that they stayed outside the fences he'd put up to keep his sheep in and Indians out. Judging from the evidence he left us, he wasn't a very exacting fence builder. Most of the thirteen miles of four- or five-wire barbed fences around and across our land are still, despite our improvements, no better than they have to be, the rusty wires and the old juniper and cedar posts holding each other up mutually. And on some sectors, we've discovered, the fence-lines do not correspond to anything in the county courthouse records. For years, according to the legal description of our place, we didn't really own our front gate, or the summit of the hill above the house; a neighboring rancher farmed some of of our land on the wrong side of the fences between us, and we grazed some of his on our side. Recently, through a series of land trades, we've "rectified our frontiers," and that's a comfort.

Our fence line must seem even more arbitrary to the deer and elk, whose immemorial trails often cross the fences at right angles, as if challenging them. As a consequence, each spring we go around with rolls of barbed wire and staples and fencing tools, and repair the considerable damage done by these wild herds jumping over or crashing through the lines. Once I found the carcass of a young buck, its limbs, head, and horns woven into the wires in a horrible knot. But usually the deer vault right over, without doing more damage than breaking or loosening a top wire or two, and so we keep on cutting and splicing and tightening our fences, and when I'm done with the job each year, I feel good about it, as if an unequal truce between the two-legs and the four-legs has been renegotiated for another year.

During the early fall hunting season, when there are still cattle on the place, we're pestered by deer hunters straying across our boundaries and sometimes cutting our fences. So like all ranchers hereabouts, we've put up signs saying POSITIVELY NO HUNTING OR TRESPASSING on prominent fence-posts facing out, for would-be trespassers and poachers to see. It's hard to say whether this posting of the property does much good, and I confess I'm not fond of putting up such blunt challenges to any and all visitors. They must seem like insults to innocent, gun-less hikers. On the other hand, most of our signs around the place are shot to pieces every few years and have to be replaced, indicating, I guess, that their message *is* reaching the right people, whether it stops them from trespassing or not. Only a few times have I ever confronted a total stranger on our lands, but others in the family have had some ugly encounters with poachers, and after one of these my father actually got himself deputized by the county sheriff, and carried a worn silver deputy's badge in his shirt-pocket during hunting season, in case he had to invoke the law.

❧

BEYOND OUR NORTHEASTERN FENCE-LINE lies another man's property, which I covet. My father could have bought this place from the son-in-law of the original homesteader, but declined, reasoning that we had enough land up here already. He was right, but coveting land is not rational, and I *do* covet this other place. It's much smaller than ours, only about eight hundred acres, but being mostly above our highest land, it's densely timbered with ponderosa pine and Douglas fir, and embellished with springs and creeks and meadows. It's not been logged in recent years, and walking through it (trespassing!) is like walking through a forest park. The blue lily-blossoms of camas appear along the creeks in June, and even in the heat of August you can always walk in the shade, and come upon little meadows full of scarlet gilia in bloom.

Once for the better part of an hour, at the edge of a meadow back in the pines, I watched a young coyote playing with a pinecone as if it were a mouse, flinging it high into the air, retrieving it with great galumphing leaps, pointedly ignoring it, and then pouncing on it again. When finally, having promises to keep, I walked into the meadow and broke the spell, the coyote ran off—but when I looked over my shoulder a few minutes later, here he came behind me, discreetly keeping his distance, fellow traveler through the woods, probably expecting me to flush out a chipmunk.

Back there at the edge of the meadow, watching the coyote at play, I had coveted nothing—what more was there to want? But later, of course, far away, I resumed my brooding over that land, and everything on it, under it, and over it, wishing that I owned it and had the undivided title to it in my safety-deposit box, and could pass it on to my children, along with our place just over the hill. For shame: thou shalt not covet thy neighbor's property, let alone his wife, and if the sin of lust applies to land as well as to human flesh, I am guilty as sin. What if I could turn my ownership-complex inside out, and really accept the proposition that the land owns me, gives me my life, requires my devoted service? The habits of thinking otherwise run very deep, but I remind myself that when Thoreau felt that universal urge to build and live in his own house, he built his Walden cabin on land he neither owned nor rented. I wouldn't want to try that now, on the shores of Walden Pond, but like everything else in Thoreau's story, it shows what you can try to do without.

Meanwhile, I keep looking for images of being in place, in the right place, without ownership. Two years ago, before he died, an old-timer here made a final request to a neighboring rancher, one of his best friends. The friend owns and flies an antique biplane, and the old-timer's wish was for his friend to take his ashes up in the old plane and scatter them over a rocky pinnacle near Trout Creek known to locals as the Dry Island. So late in spring, as the sidehills above the creek were greening, the dead man's extensive family assembled close by, and the pilot took off with his cargo and flew over the island. In the calm morning air, the old-timer's ashes came straight down in a faint ribbon of white, and vanished, reclaimed, in the bitterbrush.

NOTES

Introduction

Things were so bleak in Jefferson County in the early 1930s, according to a persistent (but undocumented) story told by old-timers, that "New Deal" technocrats in the U.S. Interior Department decided that it would make virtually the whole county a "test plot" for its "Marginal Lands" conservation project. The few remaining farmers would be relocated, presumably Madras would wither away one way or another, and the county would become in effect one vast grazing reserve. According to the story, only a desperate appeal to the Roosevelt administration by a Jefferson County leader, Howard Turner (helped out by his old friend from Oregon Trunk days, Ralph Budd, now CEO of Great Northern), prevented this drastic bit of social engineering from being enacted. What persuaded the bureaucrats especially was Turner's reminder that the government had already approved and begun preliminary work on reservoirs for the North Unit Irrigation Project in the county. So Jefferson County and the North Unit Project were spared, but in fact over 120,000 acres of "sub-marginal land" *were* reclaimed as public fee-based grazing land. My great-grandfather McCoin's homestead on Grey Butte thus became part of the "Marginal Lands" administered by the Grey Butte Grazing Association.

P. 1: Erskine Caldwell, "On the Range," *Some American People* (New York: Robert McBride Co., 1935), pp.14-16.

P. 3: W. S. Merwin, "The Last One," *The Lice* (New York: Atheneum, 1967), p. 10.

P. 4: Alexis de Tocqueville, "A Fortnight in the Woods," *Journey to America* (1829), transl. George Lawrence (London: Macmillan, 1959), p. 372.

P. 5: C. S. Luelling, *Saga of the Sagebrush Country* (1960), unpublished MS.

P. 6: William Stafford, "Allegiances," *Allegiances* (New York: Harper and Row, 1970), p. 17.

One: New Era

In its original, shorter version, this essay was first published in *Regionalism and the Pacific Northwest*, ed. William Robbins and Richard Ross (Corvallis: Oregon State University Press, 1983), pp. 175-201.

P. 22: William Stafford, "Finding Sky Ranch," first published in *Northwest Review*, Spring 1975 (14,3), 47. The poem is displayed (inscribed on a bronze placque) on a wall of the Oregon Convention Center in Portland.

Two: The Farm Boy

This essay is a revised and expanded version of "John Campbell's Adventure and the Ecology of Story," first published in *Northwest Review*, 1991 (XXIX, 2), 46-76, and reprinted in *Worldviews of the American West*, ed. Polly Stewart, Steve Siporin, C. W. Sullivan III, and Suzi Jones (Logan: Utah State University, 2000), pp. 118-134. Since completing the version included here, I've had the pleasure of working with Jim Polk Sr.'s great-grandson, George Aguilar Sr. of Warm Springs, on his forthcoming book on the family histories and traditions of the Chinookan people of Warm Springs, *When the River Ran Wild!*

Three: Around the Mountain

P. 56: H. L. Davis, "The Camp," *Kettle of Fire* (New York: William Morrow and Co., 1959), pp. 122-23.

Four: The Kiln

P. 70: G. A. Gilman, *A Practical Treatise on Lime, Hydraulic Cements, and Mortars* (New York: D. Van Nostrand, 1863), p. 127 ff.

Five: Opal City

This account of Opal City's rise and fall is based on the brief history of the community written by my mother, Wilma Mendenhall Ramsey, for *Jefferson County Reminiscences* (Portland: Binfords and Mort, 1957, 1998), pp. 239-53. I am grateful to the Bowman Museum in Prineville and the Central Oregon Community College Library in Bend, and "Family Finders" and the Jefferson County Historical Museum in Madras, for access to microfilms of articles on the Railroad Era in central Oregon newspapers.

P. 99: "Opal City," in *Oregon: End of the Trail* (Portland: Binfords and Mort, 1940), 391-92.

Six: Quincey's Ladders

A shorter version of this essay was originally commissioned by *Sports Illustrated* for a special envionmental issue, but the issue was not produced.

P. 105: Theodore Roethke, "The Lost Son," *Collected Poems of Theodore Roethke* (New York: Doubleday, 1966), p. 55.

Seven: The Canyon

This piece was inspired in part by Aldo Leopold's brilliant essay, "Thinking Like a Mountain," in *Sand County Almanac*—but I wanted to bring the same kind of environmental imagining to bear on *canyons*, central Oregon's most distinctive and widespread features. This essay in some details follows a long topographical poem I'd written earlier, "Thinking Like a Canyon," *Isle* (7, 1 (Winter 2000), 185-90.

Pp. 116-18: The information given here on the canyon's paleobotanical record owes much to the lifelong work of Mel Ashwill, of Madras, Oregon. See also Ewart Baldwin, *Geology of Oregon* (Eugene: University of Oregon Press, 1964).

P. 120: Keith and Donna Clark, "William McKay's Journal, 1866-7: Indian Scouts," Part One, *Oregon Historical Quarterly*, LXXIX, 2c (Summer 1978), 156.

P. 121: Bess Stangland Raber, *Some Bright Morning* (Bend: Maverick Publishing, 1965), p. 307.

P. 122: Lewis A. McArthur, *Oregon Geographic Names*, 3rd Edition (Portland: Binfords and Mort, 1965), p. 72.

P. 122: Russ Baehr, *Oregon's Outback* (Bend: Maverick Publishing, 1988), pp. 54-55.

Eight: Two Homesteads

The main historical source for this essay is Evada Power's account of "Hay Creek" in *Jefferson County Reminiscences* (Portland: Binfords and Mort, 1957, 1998), pp. 9-45. Birdie O'Kelley's recollections were collected by the late Martha Stranahan in 1979, and portions were published in the Redmond *Spokesman*, July 30, 1980.

Birdie's memories of attending Blizzard Ridge School #28 from 1904 to 1910 are included in Irene Helm's *Remembering School Days of Old Crook County* (Prineville: The Print Shop, 1980), p. 190:

Our teacher was Mrs. Stuart, an English lady we all liked. On nice days we had our lessons outside. At school we had the usual games of annie-over, blackman, and hide-and-seek. The lean-to at the front of the school was the cloak room, with one side for the girls and the other for the boys. We carried water from a spring somewhere nearby. There was an old Indian burial ground near the spring. I remember it scared me to look at it, but then I usually couldn't help it, I looked! It seems now that it was on a high platform, and I remember the high two-horned saddle, a skull, and old tattered shreds of a blanket, I guess, that waved in the wind.

Tom Power's narrative of growing up in Newfoundland, "Belle Island Boyhood: a Memoir of Newfoundland in the 1890's," edited by Jarold Ramsey, was published in *Newfoundland Quarterly* in Spring 1990, pp. 20-28, and Winter 1991, pp. 22-28.

Pp. 133-34: Victor Shawe's stories were featured in the *Saturday Evening Post* between 1920 and 1928; among his best are these: "Seattle Slim and the Two-Percent Solution," May 28, 1920; "McElvaney's Third One," March 14, 1925; "That Law of Lesser Concessions," July 25, 925; and "The Brown Outlaw," Nov. 14, 1925.

P. 134: *A Homesteader's Portfolio* was originally published in 1922 by Macmillan, and was reprinted, with an introduction by Molly Gloss, by the Oregon State University Press, in 1993.

P. 134: quoted by Evada Power in "Hay Creek," *Jefferson County Reminiscences*, p. 38.

Pp. 135-37: Birdie O'Kelley Palmateer, "Blizzard Ridge," *Jefferson County Reminiscences*, p. 53 ff.

Pp. 142-43: "Hay Creek," *Jefferson County Reminiscences*, pp. 40-42.

Nine: An Impromptu

First published in *Open Spaces* 5, 3 (2003), 5-7.